WHAT SOME OF VERNON COLEMAN'S READERS HAVE TO SAY

❖ 'Your willingness to say exactly what you think is a refreshing change.' P.H., HANTS

❖ 'I admire your forthright and refreshingly honest way of expressing your views and opinions...bless you for being a light in the eternal darkness.' B.O., DURHAM

❖ 'If only more people in the medical profession and this government were like you it would be a much nicer world.' G.W., HANTS

❖ 'My deep appreciation for your great courage and integrity over the years.' J.T., U.S.

❖ 'I have never before had the patience to sit down and read a book but once I started your book a few weeks ago I was riveted.' S.R., BIRMINGHAM

❖ 'I admire your direct approach and philosophy in respect of general health.' A.W., DURHAM

❖ 'It's lovely to have someone who cares about people as you do. You tell us such a lot of things that we are afraid to ask our own doctors.' K.C., NEWCASTLE

❖ 'I would like to thank you for telling us the truth' R.K., KENT.

❖ 'I feel I must write and congratulate you ... your no-nonsense attitude, teamed with plain common sense makes a refreshing change .. Please keep up the good work' L.B., LEICS

❖ 'Thanks over and over again – good health always to you as you are fighting for a good cause in life – for the sick' E.H., CLEVELAND.

❖ 'I only wish to God that we had a few such as your good self in parliament, then maybe our standard of life would possibly be better' H.H., SOMERSET.

❖ 'I must admit that initially I thought that some of your ideas were extreme, but sadly I must concede that I was wrong' C.D., SURREY

❖ 'I greatly admire your no nonsense approach to things and your acting as champion of the people' L.A., CORNWALL.

❖ 'I have now read and studied all your excellent books and have enjoyed and benefited from them immensely' B.B., DORSET.

❖ 'Your no nonsense approach to the medical profession is a tonic' C.S., TYNE & WEAR

❖ 'May I say that I think you have done a real service to all those who have the sense and patience to study your books' B.A., HAMPSHIRE

❖ 'I've just read *Bodypower* and *Food for Thought*. They will now go onto my bookshelf to be re-read many times in the future.' G.G., BUCKS

Books by Vernon Coleman

The Medicine Men (1975)
Paper Doctors (1976)
Everything You Want To Know About Ageing (1976)
Stress Control (1978)
The Home Pharmacy (1980)
Aspirin or Ambulance (1980)
Face Values (1981)
Guilt (1982)
The Good Medicine Guide (1982)
Stress And Your Stomach (1983)
Bodypower (1983)
An A to Z Of Women's Problems (1984)
Bodysense (1984)
Taking Care Of Your Skin (1984)
A Guide to Child Health (1984)
Life Without Tranquillisers (1985)
Diabetes (1985)
Arthritis (1985)
Eczema and Dermatitis (1985)
The Story Of Medicine (1985, 1998)
Natural Pain Control (1986)
Mindpower (1986)
Addicts and Addictions (1986)
Dr Vernon Coleman's Guide To Alternative Medicine (1988)
Stress Management Techniques (1988)
Overcoming Stress (1988)
Know Yourself (1988)
The Health Scandal (1988)
The 20 Minute Health Check (1989)
Sex For Everyone (1989)
Mind Over Body (1989)
Eat Green Lose Weight (1990)
Why Animal Experiments Must Stop (1991)
The Drugs Myth (1992)
How To Overcome Toxic Stress (1991)
Why Doctors Do More Harm Than Good (1993)
Stress and Relaxation (1993)
Complete Guide To Sex (1993)
How to Conquer Backache (1993)

How to Conquer Arthritis (1993)
Betrayal of Trust (1994)
Know Your Drugs (1994, 1997)
Food for Thought (1994)
The Traditional Home Doctor (1994)
I Hope Your Penis Shrivels Up (1994)
People Watching (1995)
Relief from IBS (1995)
The Parent's Handbook (1995)
Oral Sex: Bad Taste And Hard To Swallow? (1995)
Why Is Pubic Hair Curly? (1995)
Men in Dresses (1996)
Power over Cancer (1996)
Crossdressing (1996)
How To Get The Best Out Of Prescription Drugs (1996)
How To Get The Best Out of Alternative Medicine (1996)
How To Conquer Arthritis (1996)
High Blood Pressure (1996)
How To Stop Your Doctor Killing You (1996)
Fighting For Animals (1996)
Alice and Other Friends (1996)
Dr Coleman's Fast Action Health Secrets (1997)
Dr Vernon Coleman's Guide to Vitamins and Minerals (1997)
Spiritpower (1997)
Other People's Problems (1998)
How To Publish Your Own Book (1999)
How To Relax and Overcome Stress (1999)
Animal Rights – Human Wrongs (1999)
Superbody (1999)
The 101 Sexiest, Craziest, Most Outrageous Agony Column Questions
   (and Answers) of All Time (1999)
Strange But True (2000)
Food For Thought [revised edition] (2000)
Daily Inspirations (2000)
Stomach Problems: Relief At Last (2001)
How To Overcome Guilt (2001)

reports

Prostate Trouble (2000)
Vitamins and Minerals (2000)
How To Campaign (2000)

Genetic Engineering (2000)
Osteoporosis (2000)
Vaccines (2000)
Alternative Medicine (2000)

novels

The Village Cricket Tour (1990)
The Bilbury Chronicles (1992)
Bilbury Grange (1993)
Mrs Caldicot's Cabbage War (1993)
Bilbury Revels (1994)
Deadline (1994)
The Man Who Inherited a Golf Course (1995)
Bilbury Country (1996)
Second Innings (1999)
Around the Wicket (2000)

short stories

Bilbury Pie (1995)

on cricket

Thomas Winsden's Cricketing Almanack (1983)
Diary Of A Cricket Lover (1984)

as Edward Vernon

Practice Makes Perfect (1977)
Practise What You Preach (1978)
Getting Into Practice (1979)
Aphrodisiacs – An Owner's Manual (1983)
Aphrodisiacs – An Owner's Manual (Turbo Edition) (1984)
The Complete Guide To Life (1984)

as Marc Charbonnier

Tunnel (novel 1980)

with Alice

Alice's Diary (1989)
Alice's Adventures (1992)

with Dr Alan C Turin

No More Headaches (1981)

Animal Rights
Human Wrongs

The Pocket Edition

Vernon Coleman

Published by Blue Books, Publishing House, Trinity Place, Barnstaple, Devon EX32 9HJ, England.

Previously published by Blue Books under the same title in 1999. This shortened and updated edition published in 2001.

ISBN 1 899726 35 7

A catalogue record for this book is available from the British Library.

Copies of this book are being distributed to schools by Gill Readfearn of Plan 2000, 234 Summergangs Road, Hull HU8 8LL.
Tel: 01482 786855, Fax 01482 786195

Printed and bound by: J. W. Arrowsmith Ltd., Bristol

Dedication

To Alice and Thomasina. Dear, sweet friends who gave infinite joy and happiness. The only sorrow was in the parting.

This edition of *Animal Rights – Human Wrongs* is also dedicated, with grateful thanks, to Olive Coverdale who loved animals, who was an enthusiastic supporter of Plan 2000 and whose love and generosity live on and to Gill Redfearn whose tireless efforts on behalf of animals are helping to ensure that the next generation will be more caring, thoughtful and responsible than those generations who have allowed cruelty and barbarism to continue.

Acknowledgements

My thanks to the thousands of animal lovers who have written to me over the years and whose determination, honesty, bravery, perseverance and encouragement has kept alive the hope that we will and can win the war against the animal abusers. And my special thanks, as always, to Sue Ward without whose vision and understanding this book would be a much poorer creation.

Contents

Introduction

I want to see an end to cruelty to animals. I want to see animal experiments stopped. I want to be alive to celebrate the end of hunting. I want to see abattoirs closed down and car parks full of animal transport lorries, engines dead and empty of terrified sheep, cows and other creatures. I want to see all the world's farmers concentrating on growing crops (with the wonderful side effect that world hunger will immediately end). I want all this to happen soon. I want it more than I want anything else in this life. I want it more than I want greater wealth or eternal life. If Aladdin appeared before me and gave me three wishes I would improve the odds by asking for the same thing three times: an end to all cruelty.

People have been fighting for animals for centuries. But nothing positive has happened. All that effort has been to no avail. I have an irrepressible, constant suspicion that animals are treated worse now than at any time in human history.

Part of the problem has, of course, been that there has been incessant in fighting within the pro-animal movement – largely, but not exclusively, through vanity and self interest.

This is in notable contrast to what has happened within the animal abuse industry, where there has been almost constant agreement and an enthusiasm about working together which should be envied by the pro-animal movement.

Ingenuity And Imagination

Farmers, scientists and others have shown appalling ingenuity and imagination in creating an apparently endless variety of ways to abuse the other creatures with whom we share this world.

The barbarism of the Roman circuses is as nothing compared to the barbarism of the modern vivisector's laboratory, the obscenity of the modern abattoir or the cruel indecency of today's animal factory.

Slavery has stopped. Women have been emancipated. Apartheid, in all its human forms, has been roundly condemned. But the abuse of animals has accelerated.

Making The Difference

I want to be alive to see an end to cruelty to animals. I want to know that I have been part of the final thrust which has made the difference. I want to know that I have made a difference.

Of course, I can't do anything by myself – any more than you can. But I believe that we can stop animal cruelty if we work together.

If we learn everything we can from history, study our opponents' weaknesses and strengths, put aside all personal vanities (and have the courage to ignore those alleged animal supporters who take every opportunity to snipe and gripe at anyone who dares to try something new) then we will have a better chance of success than ever before.

If we sincerely and seriously want to stop animal cruelty we can.

But if we don't want it enough – and aren't prepared to put in the necessary effort – animals will continue to suffer for generations to come. Stopping the growth in cruelty to animals which has stigmatised this and previous generations, will (for reasons which I will explain in this book) become harder and harder with each year that passes.

Strange And Difficult Times

We live in strange, difficult and confusing times. In some ways – largely material – we are richer than any of our ancestors. In other ways – largely spiritual – we are infinitely poorer. Most of us live in well equipped homes that our great grand parents would marvel at. We have access to water at the turn of a tap. (Sadly, the water is deteriorating in quality and is now undrinkable.) At the flick of a switch we can obtain light to work by and heat to cook by. We have automatic ovens, washing machines, tumble driers, dish washers, food blenders, vacuum cleaners, television sets, video recorders and a whole host of other devices designed either to make our working lives easier or our leisure hours longer or more enjoyable. We can travel thousands of miles in a matter of hours.

We are surrounded by the gaudy signs of our wealth and the physical consequence of human ambition and endeavour; but loneliness, unhappiness, anxiety and depression are now commoner than at any previous time in our history. Never before has there been so much sadness, dissatisfaction and frustration as there is today. The demand for tranquillisers and sleeping tablets has steadily increased as our national and individual wealth has in

We have access to sophisticated communications systems and we n.
far more power over our environment than our ancestors ever had, and yet
we are regularly reminded of our vulnerability and our dependence on the
system we have created.

Most important of all is the fact that although we are materially wealthy
we are spiritually deprived. We have conquered most of our planet, and some
of the space which surrounds it, but we are woefully unable to live peacefully
with one another. The more control we have over our environment the more
damage we do to it. The more successful we become the more miserable we
are. The more we learn the more we forget about our duties and responsibilities
to one another.

As manufacturers and advertisers have deliberately translated our wants
into needs so we have exchanged generosity and caring for greed and self
concern. Politicians and teachers, scientists and parents have encouraged each
succeeding generation to convert simple dreams and aspirations into fiery
no-holds-barred ambitions. In the name of progress we have sacrificed
goodwill, common sense and thoughtfulness. The gentle, the weak and the
warm hearted have been trampled upon by hordes who think only of the
future. Our society is a sad one; the cornerstones of our world are selfishness,
greed, anger and hatred.

During the last fifty years or so we have changed our world beyond
recognition. With the aid of psychologists, clever advertising copywriters have
learned to exploit our weaknesses and our fears and our natural apprehensions
to help create demands for new and increasingly expensive products.
Tradition, dignity, craftsmanship, values and virtues have been pushed aside
in the search for greater productivity and profitability.

It is hardly surprising that all these changes have produced new stresses
and strains. The pressures to succeed, to conform and to acquire ensure that
the base levels of daily stress are fixed at dangerously high levels.

For twenty years it has been recognised that stress plays a vital part in the
development of most illnesses but today the fastest growing illness in the
world is something which I now call 'The 21st Century Blues' – a largely
unrecognised problem that already affects one person in three and is spreading
rapidly. The 21st Century Blues is caused by 'toxic stress'.

Toxic stress is far more destructive than ordinary stress. It is created –
often deliberately – by politicians, lawyers and advertisers and it is the cause
of much bitterness and many frustrations. It is the cause of the deep sense of
ill defined, inexplicable despair that is typical of victims of The 21st Century
Blues.

Toxic stress is the type of stress that is produced by advertisements which make you feel incompetent or inadequate ("You're a failure if you can't afford to dress like this." "You're a terrible parent if you don't buy X or Y for your children.") and it is the type of stress that is produced by lawyers who create laws which mean that however just your cause may be you won't be able to win.

The Perils Of Progress

Much of the stress from which we all suffer is created by our constant determination to progress. Our dedication to progress is one of the reasons why we have lost control of our world.

Without so much progress we would have more time to enjoy our world and our lives; without so much progress we would be better able to find happiness, contentment and stability.

But without progress industry would slow down, economic growth would be stifled and society would stand still. And that would not suit society at all. This is significant because it explains how we have created a world and a society which now control us. For the first time in history our present and our future are controlled not by us, not by our 'leaders', but by a social structure which we have devised. Our institutions and multinational corporations need progress in order to create and gain more power. The power in our world is now vested in the institutions themselves; it is the structure of our society which controls us.

Those who work for the institutions which rule our lives tell us that progress is essential but they are lying. They tell us that it is impossible to halt progress but they are lying. What they really mean is that progress is good for business, or that progress offers some advantage in terms of money or power to the part of the social structure to which they are tied. Progress is, ironically, essential to the strength of the status quo.

Most people who work for institutions and multinational corporations will insist that progress means 'better'. It doesn't. Progress means that people have to work harder and take life more seriously and it means more stress. Progress means that things become more complicated and more likely to go wrong. Progress means that the things which you bought yesterday (and were happy with until the advertisers convinced you that they were out of date) are useless within months. Progress means that new is always better and that the future is always going to be better than the past.

Progress means that more and more people have to exchange a rich and varied, wholesome and healthy lifestyle for one which is hollow and filled with despair and loneliness. Progress means deprivation for people but strength for our social structures. Progress means that the jobs people do become more boring and less satisfying. Progress means more power to institutions and to machines and computers. Progress means more stress, more destruction, more misery and more tedium. And progress means more cruelty to animals and more damage to our planet.

Are people wiser, happier and more contented now that electric toothbrushes are available? Are faster cars more satisfying than old ones? Are people more at peace than their ancestors now that the compact disc player has been invented?

The truth about progress is something of a compromise. Some advances are good. Some new technology is helpful and does improve the quality of our lives. Some new developments reduce pain, suffering and stress.

But society isn't interested in compromise. Society needs uncontrolled progress in order to grow. And the people who acquire their power and their status and their wealth from society's institutions do what they are expected to do. Our world is no longer controlled by people. It is controlled by the structure that we created.

The truth is that progress can be a boon as well as a burden. It would be as stupid to claim that all progress is bad as to claim that all progress is good. Progress is good when we use it rather than allow it to rule our lives. Progress is neither good nor bad unless we make it so.

But we no longer choose between those aspects of progress which can be to our benefit and those which may be harmful. Now that we no longer control our world we are forced to accept all progress whether we want it or not.

The Pressure Of Advertising

Whatever else you do with your life you will always be a consumer. To the multinational corporations which make items as varied as motor cars, refrigerators, underwear, indigestion remedies, biscuits, coat hangers and kitchen sinks you are a consumer.

In order to persuade you to become a customer the people who provide these products and services spend considerable amounts of money on trying to convince you that their products are better than anyone else's.

Every day your custom is solicited in a thousand different ways – some crude and some subtle. Every day you are bombarded with advertisements telling you to buy one of these and begging you to buy some of those and explaining why your life will be incomplete if you do not spend your money on a little of this and a little of that.

The professionals who prepare advertisements know very well that in order to succeed in the modern market place they must create new needs; they know that their advertising must, through a mixture of exaggeration and deceit (and through exploiting natural fears and weaknesses) create wants and desires, hopes and aspirations and then turn those wants, desires, hopes and aspirations into needs.

Multinational corporations (and their advertising agencies) know that it is impossible to sell anything to a satisfied man. But, in order to keep the money coming in (and to keep the corporate beast satisfied) the advertising agencies must constantly encourage us to buy. They constantly need to find better ways to sell us stuff that we do not really need.

Any fool can sell a product or a service that people need. If your shoes wear out then you will buy new ones or have the old ones repaired. If you are hungry and there is only one restaurant for miles then that restaurant will get your service. If you car is about to run out of petrol then a garage doesn't need to offer you free tumblers or a money off voucher for a car wash in order to win your custom.

As far as the multinational corporations are concerned the trick is to get you to buy shoes when you don't need new shoes and to buy shoes that are more expensive than they need be; to buy food when you are not hungry and to fill your car with petrol long before its tank is empty simply because you are attracted by the offer that accompanies a particular brand of fuel.

The multinational corporations want to turn your most ephemeral wants into basic needs. In order to do this their advertising agencies use all their professional skills to make you dissatisfied with what you already have. They need you to be constantly dissatisfied and frustrated. Modern advertising is a scientifically based creative art which is designed to raise the intensity of your desires and build your dissatisfaction and your fears. The advertising copywriter is hired to create unhappiness.

Multinational corporations want to take away your appreciation of the simple things in life because they know that there is more profit in making things more complicated, more expensive and more unreliable. They want you to be in so much of a hurry that you eat instant foods rather than growing and preparing your own vegetables. They want you to ride in a car rather than walk or ride a bicycle. They want to make you feel guilty if you don't smell right or don't buy the right breakfast cereal for your children. They want you to feel a failure if you don't have the latest clothes on your back and the latest gadgets in your home. Their advertising is most successful when it persuades you to forget your real needs and to replace them with wants which can then be turned into artificial needs.

Even if you don't have the money to spend on new cars, kitchen furniture, clothes and other goods so cleverly advertised you will not escape. Advertising, designed to inflame your desires, will show you services you cannot buy and things you cannot have. It will create wants and then turn those wants into needs. Advertising creates frustration and disappointment, envy and dissatisfaction. If you are too poor to buy the things which are advertised you will never discover that the products on offer are unlikely to satisfy the promises made for them.

In the hands of the multinational corporations (and their human slaves) advertising is the symbol of modern society; it frequently represents false temptations, hollow hopes and unhappiness and disenchantment; it often inspires values which are based on fear and greed. In short, the multinational corporations deliberately use advertising to make people dissatisfied and unhappy.

How Fear Creates Stress

Your ancestors lived in a world about which they understood very little and where they were constantly in danger. They had many things to be afraid of: death, pain, starvation and being eaten alive by wild animals to mention but four.

We, in contrast, should lead relatively fear-free lives.

But all the evidence firmly shows that fear plays a much bigger part in our lives than it ever played in the lives of our ancestors.

Why?

Probably because society (our unseen controller) needs us to be frightened. Fear is a powerful driving force which helps to push us forwards. Fear encourages us to accept things we do not like, to do work we do not enjoy and to spend money on things we neither want nor need. Fear cripples us but keeps us compliant. Fear is one of the most potent of all forces and it is used to control us and to manipulate our emotions.

Consider health for example.

You are encouraged to worry about your health in a thousand separate ways. Listen to the experts arguing about what is bad for you and you will soon feel twinges of fear nibbling at you. Most of the time your fears are created and maintained by people who have a vested, commercial interest in exploiting your fears so that they can sell you something.

The companies which make meat-free products tell you the virtues of not eating meat – and warn you of the hazards of eating sausages and meat pies. The people who make low-fat products warn you of the hazards of eating high-fat products. Companies selling herbal remedies tell you how dangerous doctors can be. Companies making sweeteners may warn you of the dangers of eating sugar. Companies involved in the marketing or distribution of sugar may warn you of the danger of sugar substitutes. It is not unknown for lobbyists, marketing experts and spin doctors to distort the truth in order to promote a particular message, create a special type of fear and sell a product.

Fear is everywhere and is constantly used by people who want to manipulate you. Fear isn't just used by the multinational corporations. Politicians and police chiefs frighten you about street violence in order to encourage you to give them more power. Politicians make you frightened of your enemies abroad for the same reason. (These days when politicians find themselves under pressure at home they invariably start a war abroad.) Television and radio means that you can be frightened more speedily and more effectively than ever before. Fear helps our society to sustain itself and to increase its power.

We Have Lost Control

Science fiction writers have, in the past, written about a future in which man loses power over his world because computers and robots have taken control. That hasn't happened. But we have, unthinkingly and unknowingly, lost power in a quite different way. We have lost power, and handed over control of our lives to an untouchable, nebulous, almost indefinable force. We have handed over control to institutions, organisations and multinational corporations which use our system to teach us to obey authority and which skilfully use advertising to create needs and fears.

If you carefully examine the way the world is being run at the moment you could reasonably come to the conclusion that most multinational corporations, and most governments, are more or less exclusively controlled by ruthless, James Bond villain style psychopathic megalomaniacs.

What other explanation could there be for the fact that drug companies make and sell drugs which they know are both dangerous and ineffective? What other explanation could there be for the fact that food companies make and sell food which they must know causes cancer and contains very little of nutritional value? What other explanation could there be for the fact that arms companies sell products deliberately designed to blow the legs off small children? What other explanation could there for the fact that tobacco companies continue to make, promote and sell products which they know kill a high proportion of their customers? And what other explanation could there possibly be for the fact that bureaucrats, civil servants and politicians allow all this to happen?

There is another explanation for all these things.

For the very first time in history the main opponents of justice and fair play, the proponents of abuse and tyranny, have no human form. We have created new monsters: new monsters which we cannot see or touch. (We cannot see or touch them for the excellent reason that they do not exist in reality).

For the first time in history we have succeeded in creating a world, a society, which now exists solely to defend, protect and develop itself. We have created a society whose institutions have acquired power of their own. These institutions – governments, multinational corporations, multinational bureaucracies and so on – now exist solely to maintain, improve and strengthen themselves. These institutions have their own hidden agendas and the human beings who work for them may think that they are in control but they aren't.

I now believe that the biggest threat to the survival of the human race (and the planet upon which we live) comes not from the atomic bomb, or the fact that we are steadily destroying the very fabric of our world by polluting our seas, our rivers, the air we breathe and even the space which separates us from other planets, but from the fact that we have created a social structure in which we, as human beings, now exist as mere drones. It is this new social structure which is pushing us along at a great speed and 'forcing' us not only to destroy our environment but also to abandon all those moral and ethical values which it is reasonable to expect to be fundamental in a 'civilised' society.

It may be a little difficult to accept the concept of institutions having agendas of their own but the reality is that this is exactly what has happened.

The people who appear to run large institutions, and who themselves undoubtedly believe that they are in charge, are simply institutional servants.

Consider, for example, the chairman and directors of a large multinational pharmaceutical company. These well paid men and women will regard themselves as being responsible for the tactics and strategy followed by the company for which they work. But in reality it is the company itself – an institution which only really exists on paper – which is in real control.

Every multinational company has a constant thirst for cash. In order to satisfy bankers, brokers and shareholders companies need to produce quarterly figures which show a nice big, fat profit on the bottom line.

The people who work for our imaginary drug company may think that they are in control but in reality they aren't. The directors have to do what is in their company's best interests. If they don't then their company will falter and that can't be allowed to happen. The company, the unimaginably powerful corporate demon, must come first.

So, for example, if the directors find that one of their products causes lethal side effects they may, as human beings, feel ashamed about this. Individually the directors may want to withdraw the drug immediately and to apologise to the people who have been injured by their product. But this course of action would not be in the company's best short term interests. Withdrawing the drug would doubtless cost the company money. Research and development costs would have to be written off. And apologising would expose the company to lawsuits. So the directors, acting in the company's best interests, must keep the drug on the market and deny that there are any problems. In these circumstances the company (a non-human entity which only exists on paper) is in control. The decisions are made not in the interests of people (whether they be customers or directors) but in the interests of the corporate 'being'.

The problem is compounded by the fact that, big as they are, multinational companies have no souls and no sense of responsibility. Moreover, they never think beyond the next set of quarterly figures; they are ultimately ruthless and (since they are inanimate and bloodless) utterly 'cold blooded', but they are also ultimately short sighted. Big institutions, like computers, are inherently, irretrievably, stupid. They do not realise that their behaviour will, in the long run, lead to their total destruction – partly because it will annoy and alienate their customers and partly because it will eventually result in the deaths of many of their customers.

By and large, the men and women who run large drug companies, arms companies, food companies and genetic engineering companies don't really want to destroy the world in which we all live. They know that their families have to breathe the same air as you and I. They know that they too need good food, clean drinking water and a healthy environment.

However, despite the evidence being to the contrary the people who run these companies probably think that they are doing good and useful work. They have denied the truth to themselves in order to avoid coming face to face with a reality which would probably drive them insane if they accepted it. It is only through denial and self deceit that most of the men and women who work for tobacco companies can continue to sell a product which causes so much misery and so much death. Adolf Hitler killed fewer people than the big tobacco companies have killed. But I doubt if many of the people running big tobacco companies think of themselves as evil.

I have met men and women who run large organisations (such as drug companies). Some recognise that what they are doing is immoral and they excuse themselves with such trite and shallow phrases as "If I didn't do it someone else would" and "I've got to pay the mortgage". These are, of course, variations on the same excuses favoured by the men and women who operated the gas chambers during the second world war. (The brighter and more sensitive individuals usually see through these excuses in the end; they often become depressed.)

But many men and women who work for drug companies quite honestly and sincerely believe that they are doing useful and indeed valuable work. They have become so deeply institutionalised, and are driven so completely by the needs of the corporate beast, that they genuinely feel no shame about what they do. They have rationalised their actions and denied to themselves the truths which are apparent to outside observers.

Occasionally, this constant denial and self deceit breaks down and absurdities appear. For example, British Members of Parliament have, as members of an institution, consistently voted to allow multinational corporations to pollute our drinking water and to tamper with and pollute our food. And yet MPs themselves, as individuals, are so conscious of the value of pure food and clean drinking water that in the House of Commons they have arranged to be given spring water to drink and to be fed on organic food which has not been genetically modified. The men and women who vote to allow our water to be polluted and our food to be genetically modified are voting as representatives of institutions rather than as representatives of people. They know that they are creating a world in which the food is unfit to eat and the water unfit to drink. But they can't stop it happening because they are operating for the benefit of institutions rather than people.

Suppressing The Truth

The huge organisations which now run the world have developed identities, strengths, purposes and needs of their own. And in order to continue to grow in size and in strength those organisations need to ignore or suppress as much of the truth as they can – and to ignore the truths which they cannot suppress. Obviously, the people who work for those institutions must also ignore and suppress the unpalatable truths (and they must find ways to hide from the reality of what they are doing).

How else can anyone explain the fact that huge corporations (supported by politicians) have decided to continue to damage the ozone layer – despite knowing the consequences? How else can anyone explain the fact that because antibiotics are being consistently and deliberately and knowingly used irresponsibly infectious diseases are once again a major cause of death? How else can anyone explain the fact that genetic engineers are creating foods which may or may not be safe to eat? How else can anyone explain the fact that drug companies keep on producing – and selling – products which do more harm than good?

The industrialists, the politicians and the administrators who allow these things to happen are just as vulnerable to the consequences of their actions as you and I. They – and their families – cannot buy immunity to the problems which they are creating.

The amoral but all powerful institutions we have created are not responsible for all the horrors of our world, of course. They are certainly not responsible for all the awful things we do to animals. Men and women who hunt, for example, do not hunt because they are forced to do so by an institution. They hunt because they obtain pleasure from killing and they have failed to recognise the pointless, cruel barbarism of what they do. But a very high percentage of the cruel things which we do to animals are a result of institutional needs.

For example, the continued survival of the meat trade is a result of the fact that the demands and needs of meat producing, packaging and marketing institutions have taken precedence over health and moral concerns and now have control over our lives. It has been known for decades that meat causes cancer (and a whole host of other deadly disorders). And it has also been known that if people became vegetarian and stopped eating animals world hunger would be a thing of the past simply because our resources could be used more productively.

There is no question that every human being in the world would benefit if meat eating stopped. No meat industry spokesmen would dare to debate this issue in public because they would inevitably lose.

But many large and profitable companies would go out of business if people no longer ate meat. And so the needs of the institutions take precedence over the needs of the people.

The selfish, self-centred, amoral materialism which has characterised political life for the last few decades, and which has simultaneously accompanied a downfall in morality, can no longer be seen as just another unfortunate blip in human development. The horrors of today will not be easily conquered, and will not be conquered at all unless we acknowledge the breadth and depth of the exceptional problem we now face.

Some years ago Dr Albert Schweizer saw the first signs of what has happened. "Another hindrance to civilisation today," he wrote, "is the over-organisation of our public life. While it is certain that a properly ordered environment is the condition and, at the same time, the result of civilisation, it is also undeniable that, after a certain point has been reached, external organisation is developed at the expense of spiritual life. Personality and ideas are often subordinated to institutions, when it is really these which ought to influence the latter and keep them inwardly alive."

We cannot trust our existing politicians, or the systems which they wrongly believe they control, and so what is the point of trying to persuade them to do what we want them to do – and what is right?

I have come to the conclusion that we have only one option: to take back the political power which is rightfully ours. If we are to change our world, and to replace greed and deceit with truth, kindness and courtesy we have to take action. Nothing will happen unless we want it to happen – and then make it happen. If we are to re-introduce a sense of morality into our world, and end cruelty to people and animals, we have to take back power from the institutions which now rule our lives. If we are going to take back power from the weak, spineless and unthinking politicians and corporate yes-men who serve our controlling institutions with such uncritical faithfulness we have to create our own political force. If we are to end animal cruelty then we have to recreate the way our world is run. We need a political revolution.

And that is what this book is all about.

Vernon Coleman, Devon 1999, 2001

Part One

Abuse And Hypocrisy

Chapter One

The Final Outrage

I like animals. Most of them are more intelligent, more charming, more faithful and more fun than most people and all bureaucrats.

Animals were not made for human beings to use any more than women were made for male amusement, or black people were made to work for white people. The struggle for freedom for animals is as important a struggle as any struggle ever fought. Animal abuse is the last great outrage and yet most people are so accustomed to the excruciating suffering of animals that they take little or no notice. They comfort themselves with the false belief that animals have no feelings and, therefore, do not suffer.

Animals — and other non-human creatures — are treated with no more respect than grass, rocks or ripples on a pond. Non-human creatures are regarded as outsiders with no rights other than to serve our human purposes. They may be (and are) beaten, tortured, humiliated, maimed, starved, imprisoned, robbed of their dignity, chased and killed for fun, boiled or skinned alive, eaten and generally abused. Non-human creatures — however wise, however sensitive — are regarded as mere commodities, to be bought and sold like oranges or gold or ears of wheat. Humans seem to take a perverted delight in thinking of new ways to abuse the inhabitants with whom they share this planet.

Signposts To The Nature Of The Human Spirit

People are at their truest when treating animals. The man who is a bully to other human beings will bully his dog. The man who is kind to animals will be kind to people. The way we treat animals provides signposts to the nature of the human spirit.

Many people refer to the animals with whom they share their homes as 'pets' but I do not like the image it portrays. Animals are not pets and we do not own them. We share a world together, that is all. We give and we receive.

The animal abusers rule in our society because they are violent and aggressive people. Their illusions and prejudices dominate our society. The rude, the selfish, the ruthless, the bigoted, the cruel, the intolerant, the hard hearted, the hateful and the savage have conquered the earth. The world is divided into two sorts of people: the sensitive and the insensitive. The sensitive suffer for everyone. They don't hurt other creatures but they suffer the pain for the harm done by the insensitive. Hunters, vivisectors, butchers and so on are the insensitive, brutal barbarians of our society.

The animal abusers are the ultimate narrow-minded, tunnel-visioned provincials; full of arrogance and misconceptions. Savage tribes were provincial in that they regarded all strangers as barbarians to be robbed or eaten or both. Today the animal abusers are the ultimate provincials. They do not see or accept that we do not have unique rights over the world but that we must share it with those other creatures who live upon it.

Prejudices – Ancient And Modern

Back in Roman times any non Roman who committed a heinous crime against a Roman would be executed. If a slave trod on his master's foot he would lose his head. But a Roman could commit any crime against a non-Roman without fear of retribution. This happened because the Romans saw themselves as the centre of the universe.

The Greeks felt much the same as the Romans did in that a Greek could do more or less what he liked to a slave but a slave would be punished severely if he offended a Greek.

And the same is, of course, true of the Jews.

The Romans, the Greeks and the Jews (and many other groups of people) behaved in this way because they had not grown out of their primitive, barbaric view of the world. They never really imagined that their victims could suffer in the same way that they could. They did not think of their victims as having senses, or of being capable of thought. A slave was much like a sandal – something to be bought, used and thrown away when no longer wanted.

In modern times white Americans, South Africans and Australians have all behaved in the same way when dealing with black people. They behaved in this way partly because they had not evolved away from their barbaric origins and partly because white men and women felt that to give black people rights would be economically inconvenient. They protected themselves against the absurdity of this crass reasoning by refusing to acknowledge that black people could think, or reason or suffer.

And, of course, for centuries men of all races have behaved in a similar way towards women – refusing to give them equality and arguing that this was excusable because women were not equal.

Blind Egoists

The way in which human beings now exploit and abuse animals (and other living creatures) is no different in principle to the way in which the Romans treated their slaves, the Americans treated non-white races and the Victorian Englishman treated 'his' women.

In every case the underlying problem is the same: the exploiters see the world from a provincial, small minded standpoint. Those who exploit have inherited from barbarians and savages the utterly self centred belief that they – and they alone – are blessed with wisdom and imagination. They are narrow-minded, bigoted bullies, blind egoists who cares only about themselves and their own tiny world. And they try to support their bigotry and their prejudices with pseudo-scientific nonsenses which bear no resemblance to the truth.

The black man was regarded as having no rights other than to serve the white man. The sheep is regarded as having no rights other than to serve mankind.

People who like animals, and who have been sickened by the barbaric way evil-spirited farmers, tyrannical scientists and other barbarians exploit them, have been campaigning against the establishment and for animal rights for a long, long time. Two and a half thousand years ago Buddha taught that it is as bad for a man to murder a sheep as to murder his father. ("Both equally love life and fear death. In this there is no difference.") After all murder is murder is murder is murder.

Those who love animals are widely regarded (particularly by politicians, scientists and pseudo-intellectuals) as irrational, sentimental, Bambi-hugging bunny lovers. The gentle and the humane have for too long been regarded as merely weak and ineffectual.

The laws and regulations which currently exist to 'protect' animals are conveniently designed so as not to inconvenience humans. The laws and regulations governing the use of animals in experiments are so weak and ineffectual, and so poorly policed, that they might as well not exist. The laws authorise cruelty and oppression more than they try to prevent it. Our laws relating to animals are a sheer disgrace. Experimenters can cause whatever pain they like to animals as long as the cage in which the tortured animal will be imprisoned afterwards is a certain modest size. To make life easy for the animal abusers there are so many exceptions to the rules, and so few 'checks' to make sure that the rules are being obeyed, that even the regulations which do exist are little more than cosmetic in nature.

Laws which exist to stop hunters shooting animals are usually only there to make sure that the animals in question are not wiped out completely. (Although in France when hunters were asked whether or not they would approve of a ban on hunting during "la periode de reproduction animale" a headline in the newspaper *Le Monde* announced that 79% of hunters would agree to respect a ban during this period. No one seemed perturbed, surprised or even alarmed by the fact that if you look at this survey the other way it shows that 21% of hunters are so short of functioning cerebral tissue that they wanted to continue to kill animals during the breeding season too. The hunters did not even understand that if you stop animals from breeding you soon won't have any animals left at all.)

Chapter Two

Three Varieties Of Abuse

Animals are sensitive and emotionally labile creatures who experience the same kinds of feelings that humans experience: happiness, sadness, hope, fear, love, compassion and shame.

Cruelty to animals is a moral and ethical outrage; it is the greatest crime of our time. And yet animals are abused today in three main ways: the meat industry, vivisection and hunting.

The Meat Industry

Farmers breed animals, stuff them into lorries and transport them for days without providing anything for them to eat or drink.

We cage them in tiny boxes, move them about soaked in their own urine and knee deep in their own excrement, scare them senseless and then slit their throats and eat them – tonsils, intestines, shit and all.

Next time you're on a journey keep an eye open for a lorry taking animals to a slaughterhouse. It doesn't matter where you are, where you've been or where you are going – the movement of animals is now big business. All over the world animals are constantly on the move.

There probably won't be anything printed on the side of the lorry to tell you what is in inside, but the lorry will have wooden, slatted sides and through the gaps you will be able to see the terrified faces of cows, sheep, chickens and other living creatures being transported from farm to abattoir. There may be a leg or two sticking out in between the slats because the animals will have almost certainly been herded into lorries without either respect or care.

The lambs and calves crammed into transporter lorries are just as terrified as any child would be under those circumstances. Their mothers are just as much in mourning as any mother would be. When slaves were transported from one nation to another they were branded and herded into overcrowded containers. We do the same thing with animals today.

The animals are crammed into the lorries so tightly that if they get stuck in a difficult position they have to stay that way until the journey stops many days later.

Imagine how you would feel if you had to travel for 24 hours with one of your legs sticking out through a slightly open car window. Imagine it. Think about it. The horror in these transporters is so great that the spiritual stench of it clings to the woodwork and the metalwork. If you are sensitive to animals you can feel and hear the pain and the fear whenever one of these trucks comes near. While travelling recently I stopped at a petrol station where an animal transport lorry was parked. As I got out of my car I heard the plaintive, heart wrenching cries of the sheep inside it. I filled my tank, paid at the kiosk and then felt myself drawn irresistibly, and against my will, towards the lorry. To my astonishment when I looked inside the lorry was empty. The cries I had heard had been real. But there were no animals in the lorry.

To make matters worse the animals being transported invariably travel in tiers. The more animals you can cram into a lorry the bigger the profit will be. And although animals aren't usually fed or watered while they are travelling animals, like all living creatures, need to pass urine and faeces from time to time. In a way the animals on the top tier are relatively lucky, I suppose. The animals underneath are constantly showered with urine and faeces raining down upon them from the terrified creatures above them.

Moving and killing animals is big business but it is also a truly barbaric business. Animals die, unattended and uncared for where they have fallen. Some sheep freeze to death in winter and some die from heat exhaustion and thirst in summer. As long as the numbers who die don't rise so high that the transportation process becomes unprofitable no one cares.

Animals may be moved about many times – so that farmers, transport people and meat companies can make money from cross border subsidies. Animals are shipped from steel pen to auction house to steel pen to slaughterhouse. Thousands of animals die from 'shipping fever'. Sheep and lambs are so stressed that they collapse and die. Chickens are packed into tiny cages. Pigs have their tails cut off (without an anaesthetic, of course) to prevent stress induced tail biting. Animals shipped to the Middle East are eventually killed in a brutal ritualistic style of slaughter.

The people who are involved in moving and killing animals are truly the dregs of our society. These are the sort of people who would have happily operated German gas chambers during the second world war.

250,000 Murders Every Hour

Animal transport is big business because millions of animals are slaughtered every day for the meat trade. Approximately 2,000,000 animals are murdered every working day in British abattoirs alone. That's 250,000 murders every hour, 4,167 murders every minute and 69 murders every second.

Animals are supposed to be stunned before they are killed – so that they aren't conscious when their throats are cut. But stunning is a pretty ineffective business. The people who do it aren't trained – not, at least, in a way that I would regard as proper training – and too many animals are conscious and terrified when they are killed. (It is surely not irrelevant that more than half the abattoir owners in Britain have a criminal record.)

Moreover, there is now evidence to show that the electric shock which is allegedly used to knock animals unconscious may fail to work properly. Even after they have been stunned animals do feel intense pain. They are paralysed. But they can feel pain.

Even if stunning worked well not all animals would benefit for not all animals are stunned before killing.

The law allows Jews to slaughter all the animals they kill without stunning them first. It is called ritual slaughter. Some ritual. Think about this: the animals killed for consumption by Jews are quite conscious when their throats are cut. This is such a barbaric ritual that I'm surprised there isn't someone dancing around in war-paint and feathers while the killing is being done. In Britain around 60,000 cows and calves, 30,000 sheep and lambs and 2,500,000 hens are killed by Jewish slaughterers every year. Since not all the meat obtained from killing animals the Jewish way is eaten by Jews the meat which is left over can be sold for ordinary consumption. So, whether you are Jewish or not, if you eat meat there is a good chance that the meat you buy comes from an animal which was killed in this truly cruel and barbaric way.

How Jews can support what happens in slaughterhouses in their name I do not understand. I cannot imagine that any god could possibly condone such activities.

(This has, incidentally, absolutely nothing whatsoever to do with race or religion. I will undoubtedly be accused of being anti-Semitic by bigots who do not understand that my objection to ritual slaughter has nothing to do with religion and everything to do with respect for animals.)

"It is often said that if slaughterhouses were made of glass most people would be vegetarians," wrote Jeffrey Masson and Susan McCarthy in their vitally important book *When Elephants Weep*, adding that: "If the general public knew what went on inside animal experimentation laboratories, they would be abolished."

But, as Masson and McCarthy point out slaughterhouses are virtually invisible because that is what the public want. People know what goes on inside abattoirs but they do not want to be reminded of the horrors perpetrated in their name.

Enough To Make You Proud

Imagine.

You are taken from a field where you are living with your family. You are separated from your surroundings and your loved ones and you are crammed into a lorry. You are then driven for hours in discomfort, without food or water and in a constant rain of urine and faeces to a slaughterhouse. There you are kept waiting – afraid and uncertain.

Finally, you are taken into a blood stained building where your throat is cut. You then slowly bleed to death, terrified, confused, and in pain. It may take you minutes to die.

Doesn't it all make you proud to be human. Proud to be a member of the Master Species?

Brutal, Crude And Merciless

The butcher's shop is the ultimate human disgrace; as much an indignity to man himself as it is to the slaughtered creatures whose blood decorates its every surface; their skinless corpses hung, as though with pride, from hooks in the window.

Walking past a window in which skinned corpses are displayed is nauseating. Every sensitive council should immediately pass a law insisting that butchers cover up their windows and serve their awful wares behind closed doors.

I have no doubt that if there was a market for such delicacies the crude, ruthless and mindless 'people' who operate and work in these shops would happily sell babies' brains, young boys' hearts, breasts sliced from teenage girls' bony chests and feet hacked from young mothers. Butchers are, inevitably, a hard-hearted group: insensitive and bloodthirsty, with no redeeming features. Given half a chance they would happily sell the corpses of the elderly, brought fresh from the killing rooms of hospitals and hospices in their neighbourhood. Jean Jacques Rousseau, the French philosopher, argued that butchers (whose daily trade is death and who cannot, therefore, be regarded as being blessed with the normal quota of compassion) should not be allowed to sit on juries or testify in court.

Butchers are a dying breed. Good riddance to them all.

Farming, too, is a brutal, crude, merciless business.

Chicks never see a hen and hens are kept in tiny battery cages. (Those who eat eggs often argue that hens lay more eggs than they can hatch. But hens exhaust themselves by laying so many eggs simply because their eggs are taken away from them.) Dairy cows are artificially inseminated. As soon as they give birth their calf is ripped away from them. Calves are kept chained in tiny stalls and fed on a chemical rich diet for veal production. The mother's milk is sucked out along rubber tubes and sold by the massive dairy industry.

Farmers defend the practice of taking milk from cows by arguing that without its calf the cow has milk to spare. They do not question their right to take the calf from the cow. They argue that the calf can be given other food. They do not understand that no milk is as good for a calf as its mother's milk. They continue to pump the milk out of the cow until the poor creature becomes weakened, and exhausted.

Sheep are forced to breed at an unusual and unhealthy rate so that their lambs can be sold for extra profit. And sheep are shorn not only in the early summer (when they may be hot and uncomfortable and welcome a few months without a heavy fleece) but also, quite cruelly, during the winter when they need the warmth their own wool provides.

A Contemptible Breed

Like many sentient individuals I loathe farmers. I regard them as a contemptible breed with more front than Blackpool and with as poorly developed a sense of personal responsibility as modern politicians.

When, entirely through own stupidity and greed, they created the Mad Cow crisis their instinctive reaction was not to apologise to their customers, or to wring their hands and beg forgiveness, but to demand compensation from the government.

The Mad Cow scandal should have awakened us all to the fact that most farmers – like the rest of the huge army of slimy good for nothings involved in the dead animal business – are pustulant, crooked, self-centred, stupid and greedy, concerned only with their own profits.

But the eternally damned farmers are so skilful at manipulating politicians and the media that they have actually managed to make many people feel sorry for them.

Open your newspaper or turn on your television set and you will probably discover that the farmers, the butchers and the abattoir workers are, yet again, bleating about financial losses, redundancies and bleak futures.

"We have screwed up yet again so you will have to give us money to make sure that we don't suffer financially" is the oft repeated communal cry from terror stained farmyards all over the nation.

And the government, accustomed to handing out taxpayers' money to rich farmers, immediately complies.

"Whoops, oh dear," the politicians cry. "How terrible for you. How much money would you like? Will it be all right if we send round a lorry load of the stuff on Thursday?"

"Send the lorry direct to the bank," say the farmers wearily. "We can't be bothered to handle it ourselves."

You will, of course, have noticed that the individuals who contracted Mad Cow Disease were not offered compensation by the farmers who were responsible for creating the problem.

Manipulative Money Grabbers

For years now farmers, and others involved in the meat business, have taken risks with the lives of those who buy their products simply to make an extra few billion pounds profit.

It was the farmers – manipulative money grabbers that they are – who chose to feed their animals with the food which created Mad Cow Disease. Years ago those in the animal murdering business could have protected themselves – and the meat eating world – from the horrors of Mad Cow Disease. They could have taken tougher, stricter action. But they didn't. They – and the government – falsely insisted that there wasn't a problem.

Even if they didn't know for certain that there was a problem coming (and I think they should have known) they should have realised that there was a big risk.

What would happen if any other businessman cut corners, took risks with his customers' lives and caused widespread panic and chaos? Would he expect his customers to pay for all his losses and give him compensation to make sure that he didn't lose any money? Or would he start looking for a sharp lawyer to protect him against the lawsuits that he knew would soon start thudding through his letterbox?

Why are farmers (and the rest of the meat industry) treated in such a special way? Why were the people in the animal murdering business pitied during and after the Mad Cow Disease fiasco? Why did the taxpayer have to help them out? Why did you and I have to fork out our hard earned cash to pay for their greed inspired error? In short, why, in the name of a blood soaked abattoir worker's apron, were Britain's farmers given compensation for this self created problem?

If the weather is bad does the government bale out the tourist industry? If village shops are put out of business by new superstores are they compensated? (These are, you will note, not problems which are self created. And nor are these industries which cause mass murder. Inexplicably, it seems that governments prefer to help an industry which causes its own problems and is responsible for an uncountable number of deaths.)

If you buy a lottery ticket and you don't win do you expect the government to refund your stake money? If your house is worth less than you paid for it a few years ago are you going to go running to the government for financial help?

The farming industry created Mad Cow Disease by turning herbivores into carnivores (actually, into cannibals). It was their financial problem – not ours. But the animal abusers have a huge amount of power over the current political system.

Ignorance, Stupidity And Greed

Apart from trying to feed us beef, milk and lamb contaminated with Mad Cow Disease our farmers have been working hard to ensure that our meat contains plenty of chemicals, drugs and hormones, that many of our eggs are infected and that just about everything that comes fresh from the farm will be contaminated with chemical sprays, fertilizers and pesticides.

The overuse of antibiotics on farms has helped create a world in which infections are now rapidly increasing.

I also believe that the reckless use of other drugs and hormones has contaminated farm products for decades. The over use of fertilisers, pesticides and other chemicals has polluted our water supplies and poisoned thousands of consumers.

(There is some irony in the fact that although the tobacco industry has had to put warnings on its products, farmers – the other major cause of cancer in our modern society – just get bigger and bigger subsidies.)

By getting rid of hedgerows and spraying their deathly crops with chemicals farmers have managed to do irreparable damage to our wildlife.

So, it is clear, if you want to win government support you simply have to screw up people's health, kill millions of animals in as cruel a way as possible and cause irreparable damage to the environment. Politicians will then give you whatever you ask for.

Today, farmers are messing around with genetically manipulated animals and crops because they see more ways to increase their profits. They don't give a damn that they are playing a dangerous game and that they are likely to produce permanent and terrifying changes in our world. Farmers don't give a fig for your health or your children's health. All they care about is profits.

A Doomed Trade

The meat trade is doomed. There is now 24 carat gold evidence available to show that people who eat meat are far more likely to get cancer and die young.

(Indeed, since it is impossible to be sure that the animal the meat eater consumes doesn't itself have cancer there is a good chance that the nice juicy steak into which the meat eater tucks with such relish could well contain a nice juicy lump of cancer in the middle of it. "How do you like your cancer cooked, sir?" "Mustard with your fried cancer, madam?")

Eating meat is bad for you and bad for the rest of the world too. When the meat trade is finished there will never again be any need for human beings to starve. Feeding cattle uses up vast quantities of grain and good land and meat eaters are directly responsible for the starving millions in Africa and Asia.

Perhaps, in a few years time restaurants will have meat eating sections and vegetarian sections in the same way that they now have smoking and non smoking sections. The meat eaters will be crammed at the back in dark and dingy corners.

Meanwhile, those of us who want to change the world, should remind meat eaters that if they eat bits of animal flesh they cannot be practising Christians, Catholics or Jews. (The bible says: "flesh with the life thereof, which is the blood thereof, shall ye not eat." Does anyone seriously believe that even the barbaric Jewish method of killing can empty every drop of blood from an animal's body?).

Abuse In The Name Of Science

We also abuse animals in the name of science.

Every thirty seconds another thousand animals are tortured to death in laboratories around the world. Cats, kittens, puppies, dogs, monkeys, rats, hamsters: you name the species they torture it and kill it. How much difference is there between performing an experiment on a primate and performing the same experiment on a child?

The scientists who perform animal experiments, and their supporters, claim that what they do helps human beings. This is, of course, a lie. The evidence shows quite clearly that no animal experiment ever helped a human being. Moreover, animals are so completely different to people that experiments on animals are dangerously misleading. I find it impossible to escape the conclusion that thousands of experiments have been conducted on animals for money, personal advancement or intellectual curiosity.

It is disingenuous to claim that scientists are any different to barbarians watching cock-fighting, bull-fighting or other spectacles of abuse. What difference is there between those who torment animals in the name of science and the sort of people who abuse children, beat their wives or bully the weak?

Drug companies use animal experiments to get new products on the market without testing them properly. If tests show that a new drug causes cancer in five animal species the company will dismiss the evidence as irrelevant – because animals are different to people. But, apparently without embarrassment or shame, they will then use the one experiment which shows that their new drug doesn't cause cancer in a sixth species to get their product on the market.

Cosmetic companies use animals in a variety of ways. Countless rabbits have had chemicals dropped into their eyes in pointless and unnecessary 'toxicity' tests. But it is in so-called 'medical research' that animals are most widely used. And it is 'medical research' which so often provides the excuse for the terrible things researchers do to animals.

Primates are killed so that hunters can capture their infants and sell them to British vivisectors who are paid with money contributed by British taxpayers.

Special breeding facilities produce millions of mice, rabbits, rats, cats and other animals. The animals are kept in small, sterile cages – separated from one another's comfort.

The people who perform experiments on animals are largely incompetent and stupid. Their experiments are always worthless and often badly done. Successive British Home Secretaries have protected vivisectors by claiming that all applications for licences to experiment on animals should be treated as 'confidential'. The result has been that those who oppose animal experiments have never had the opportunity to question the validity of experiments before they have started.

It is hardly surprising that, with drug companies relying so heavily on animal experiments, at least one in six people in hospital are there because they have been made ill by doctors.

Vivisectors receive vast amounts of money (much of it provided by drug companies but a good deal of it provided by the government) but have produced consistently worthless results. The only consistent factor about animal experiments is their pointlessness.

Some years ago I conducted a survey of British doctors which showed a great scepticism about, and disapproval of, animal experiments. Here is a summary of the results of that survey:

❖ 88% of doctors agreed that laboratory experiments performed on animals can be misleading because of anatomical and physiological differences between animals and humans.

❖ 81% of doctors agreed that they would like to see scientists trying harder to find alternatives to animals for testing drugs and cosmetics.

❖ 51% of doctors agreed that patients would suffer fewer side effects if new drugs were tested more extensively on human cell and tissue cultures.

❖ 69% of doctors agreed that too many experiments on animals are performed.

Despite many claims to the contrary, vivisectors regularly break guidelines for animal care. I have in my possession a photograph of a monkey in a laboratory which has the word 'crap' written on its forehead. Vivisection is nothing more than a form of pseudoscientific black magic whose practitioners have promised much but who have in reality constantly obstructed medical progress. It is no coincidence that vivisectors frequently refer to the animals they torture and kill as being 'sacrificed'.

I believe that vivisectors – and there are 20,000 in Britain alone – are the sort of people who have in the past enjoyed experimenting on blacks or Jews. If society currently allowed it I have no doubt that vivisectors would happily take Jews and the mentally ill into their laboratories instead of (or, as well as) baboons and chimpanzees.

What difference is there in the mental make up of a serial murderer and a vivisector? And yet vivisectors often expect, claim (and receive) respect in our society. Those who oppose vivisection are expected to prove that animal experiments are unnecessary and without scientific value. In any sane and just world it would be the job of the vivisectors to prove that their work was essential and valuable. (Something they would not, of course, be able to do.)

The vivisectors' entirely false claims that their barbarous and merciless experiments are of value (and their utterly immoral argument that the end justifies the means) are accepted without question because to question them would be to force ourselves to face difficult and painful truths.

Vivisection is totally supported by just about every section of the British establishment. Organisations which oppose vivisection are denied charitable status whereas organisations which have charitable status, and can, therefore, claim all the associated tax benefits, are allowed to campaign vigorously for vivisection – and perform vivisection too! What sort of world is it which gives special charitable status to organisations which abuse animals and yet denies charitable status to organisations which want to save animals?

I've been arguing for a complete ban on animal experiments for years. The supporters of vivisection now refuse to debate with me for one very simple reason: they always lose. A couple of years ago I began a guest appearance on a two hour long nationwide radio programme by challenging vivisectors and vivisectionists to name one disease for which a cure had been found through vivisection. Despite the fact that many vivisectionists telephoned the programme not one managed to come up with a disease for which vivisection had been an essential or integral part of the research process. I wasn't surprised. Vivisection is useless, always has been useless and always will be useless.

I loathe and despise scientists who perform animal experiments. I think they are truly beyond understanding, forgiveness or redemption. I believe they are the grown up, authorised versions of those evil eyed, spotty faced children who somehow obtain warped, distorted pleasure from pulling the wings off flies or peppering passing cats with airgun pellets.

Who, other than vivisectors, could argue that animals do not cry or moan or whimper in pain but are merely 'vocalising'?

How could any sane, sentient being not feel disgusted by what goes on in animal research laboratories? There can be no moral or ethical justification for the legalised mayhem which, worldwide, results in the slow, painful destruction of around 1,000 dogs, cats, kittens, puppies, monkeys, rabbits and other animals every thirty seconds. In Britain, where around 3 million experiments are performed every year on cats, kittens, dogs, puppies and other animals there are just 21 inspectors to make sure that vivisectors obey what rules exist about animal treatment.

The Home Office claims that the effectiveness of this tiny group of inspectors: "depends upon ability to gain the respect and cooperation of the scientific community as, to function, inspectors must have unfettered access to the current and future plans of scientists".

This seems as odd to me as a statement that the effectiveness of the police: "depends upon the ability to gain the respect and cooperation of the criminal community as, to function, inspectors must have unfettered access to the current and future plans of criminals".

Why, I wonder, should vivisectors, arch animal abusers, be treated with such tenderness?

A Hollow Excuse

The excuse which is always offered for this evil business is that animal experiments help doctors treat human patients more effectively.

"If it's the health of my kid or the lives of a thousand cats and dogs then the dogs and cats have to be sacrificed," said one young father I know.

"Why would scientists do animal experiments if they weren't useful?" demanded a misguided young mother. "I don't want to know what they do," she added quickly. "But I'm sure they wouldn't do what they do if it wasn't necessary."

Those who believe that animal experiments are useful exhibit a rather pathetic mixture of ignorance and naivety. They don't want to know the facts because the facts are too awful to contemplate.

Ignorance And Naivety

The ignorance and naivety is widespread.

One BBC producer refused to broadcast an interview in which I had described experiments involving dogs. "They didn't use dogs," the producer apparently said after talking to the people who had done the experiments. "They only used dog tissue."

The sad and savage but, I believe, undeniable truth is that no experiment performed on an animal has ever saved a human life. Animal experiments are so unreliable that no doctor with a brain larger than a pea would ever trust any so called evidence obtained by an animal researcher.

On the contrary, I believe that animal experiments are not only entirely useless but that they are a major cause of human illness, misery and death.

The evidence for these stout and possibly startling assertions is not difficult to find.

I can give you the names of dozens of frequently prescribed drugs – widely used around the world – which are known to cause cancer or other serious diseases when given to animals.

But this evidence is ignored because doctors know damned well that the fact that a drug causes cancer in an animal has no relevance to human beings.

When a drug company tests a new drug on animals it does so because it cannot lose. If the experiment shows that the drug does not kill the animal the drug company can claim that its tests have shown the drug to be safe. On the other hand if the experiment shows that the drug does kill the animal the drug company will dismiss the research evidence on the grounds that animals are different to people. The drug companies win every time. People (and the animals, of course) are the innocent losers.

Animal experiments are done because they are useful – to the drug companies not people. Animal experiments give drug companies no-lose evidence which will be accepted by governments around the world.

Drug companies know that extensive testing on human beings would be costly and time consuming. More important: many new drugs would never obtain a licence for widespread use if the pre-launch tests on people were too extensive (because dangerous and possibly lethal side effects would undoubtedly be discovered at an embarrassingly early stage).

If animal experiments were banned the drug companies would lose billions of pounds a year in lost revenue.

The thousands of scientists who perform and support animal experiments will deny all this, of course.

What else are they to do?

You can hardly expect them to admit that their evil but well paid work is inspired by corporate greed and self interest rather than more noble motives.

The fact is that they do not have the strength of spirit to turn their backs on the big money offered by the drug companies. And many know that if they admit that animal experimentation is flawed beyond redemption they will be admitting that they have wasted their lives.

Some of them undoubtedly want to believe their own propaganda. Those who possess some vestige of a conscience probably only sleep by denying to themselves the horror of what they do.

Scorned, Laughed At, Ruined And Imprisoned

History is full of examples of original thinkers who have been scorned, laughed at, ruined and imprisoned for daring to be creative and original and (most heinous a crime of all) for having the temerity to question (and therefore threaten) the status and authority of the establishment.

Socrates was condemned to death for being too curious. Dante was condemned to be burned at the stake. The works of Confucius were still banned in China two and a half thousand years after his death. Spinoza was denounced for being independent and every schoolchild knows about Galileo's battles with the Church. Paracelsus was the greatest influence on medical thinking since Hippocrates but the establishment regarded him as a trouble maker and persecuted him all around Europe. (He is still regarded with considerable fear and distaste by the medical establishment which, on the whole, prefers not to acknowledge his existence or his importance).

Semmelweiss, the Austrian obstetrician was ostracised by the medical profession for daring to criticise filthy medical practices. Thoreau was imprisoned for sticking to his ideals. Wilbur and Orville Wright were dismissed as hoaxsters by the Scientific American, the US Army and most American scientists. When Wilhelm Röntgen discovered X rays his achievement was described as an elaborate hoax by one of Britain's most eminent scientists.

The relationship between a diet low in vitamin C and the development of scurvy was first described in 1636 by John Woodall. James Lind reintroduced the idea in 1747 but it wasn't until 1795 that the British Admiralty decreed that lime juice should be part of every sailor's diet. Only God can possibly know how many sailors died as a result of this appalling example of cooperative prejudice.

The inventors of turbine power, the electric telegraph, the tank, the electric light, television and space travel were all laughed at or ignored by the scientific establishment. William Reich's books were burned by the Nazis in the 1930s and by the American government in the 1950s. (The Federal Food and Drug Administration was still burning his books in 1960).

More recently Dr Dean Ornish, who was responsible for devising a safe, effective treatment programme for heart disease that depends upon a vegetarian diet, exercise and relaxation was denied funds by the American National Institutes of Health and the American Heart Association.

The irony about science (which is ostensibly a search for new truths) is that most members of any scientific establishment seem dedicated to opposing real progress and suppressing original thought. There is room for original thought and originality in most areas of intellectual thought except science; the one area which one might suppose would depend almost exclusively upon original thinking.

One can attack existing political or economic theories with some freedom but any scientist with a new and original idea is likely to be regarded as a dangerous crank rather than an original scientist whose ideas may be worth evaluation.

When I said on the radio recently that I thought that it was vital to maintain an open mind another panellist on the same programme commented that in his view: "Open minds are empty minds."

This grossly prejudiced viewpoint is quite common among many of the world's best known scientists and, together with a misplaced sense of professional loyalty, helps to explain why the vast majority of new and original ideas are dismissed out of hand, and their authors sneered at and dismissed as cranks and nutcases.

Anyone who opposes the use of animals in experiments will be marginalised and dismissed as out of step with the scientific establishment. The fact that the scientific evidence shows, without any doubt whatsoever, that animal experiments are entirely worthless, does not seem to be regarded as relevant by the illogical and prejudiced supporters of vivisection. They have each taken their thirty pieces of silver and are loyal to their paymasters.

More Than Just An Evil Abuse

Animal experimentation is the most evil manifestation of animal abuse. Even if it were useful I would oppose it on moral and ethical grounds.

But animal experimentation is more than just an evil abuse of animals (terrible though that is). It is one of the main reasons why doctors are now as big a cause of illness and death as are cancer and heart disease. Animal experiments are not merely part of a major scientific cock-up. They are part of a huge, international conspiracy. The aim is simply to make money. And the price – the lives of millions of animals and people – is considered acceptable. Remember: animal experiments kill people as well as animals.

(It is interesting to note that animal experiments may sometimes be performed in order to enable companies to continue damaging human beings. For example, dogs, who would never voluntarily choose to do anything so stupid and self-damaging, were forced to smoke cigarettes in bizarre and utterly pointless experiments. I have a suspicion that these experiments were done to show that the tobacco companies were generously using their own money in order to investigate the links between tobacco and cancer while at the same time holding back the moment at which it would have to be admitted that tobacco did cause cancer in humans. Animal experiments are often used in this way.)

Those who support the use and abuse of animals in the name of science will, it seems, stop at nothing. I have spent most of my life campaigning against injustices to human beings and animals and have become accustomed to attempts at intimidation but none of my campaigns have ever attracted quite so much violent, uncontrolled, snarling hostility as my campaign to stop animal experiments.

I oppose the use of animals in laboratory experiments – one of the great growth industries of our time – for numerous reasons.

I believe with all my heart and soul that animal experiments are morally, scientifically and ethically wrong. What right can scientists possibly have to torture, burn and cut animals of other species? What excuse can there be for such obscene cruelty?

We should never forget that in the false name of science one thousand kittens, cats, puppies, dogs, monkeys, rabbits and other animals are tortured and murdered every thirty seconds. They are isolated, subjected to agonising pain, ignored, maltreated and left to die in laboratories around the world. By any standards of morality this must be wrong.

It is all made worse by the fact that animal experiments are totally useless and of no use to anyone concerned with scientific truth. If vivisection were stopped tomorrow it would never be introduced again because no one would ever be able to find an argument supporting its introduction. Animal experiments are so barbaric and so unsupportable on moral, ethical, scientific or medical grounds that once they are stopped no one will ever dream of letting them start again. Vivisection is the greatest abuse of our time and I find it difficult to understand the minds of those who practise and support this evil activity.

The only reason that vivisection has not yet been stopped is that the battle of words has to be fought not just against waves of commercially sustained prejudice but also against apparently endless seas of ignorance and indifference.

Animal experiments are done in our names. Those who have done nothing to stop this evil, barbaric and pointless cruelty do not deserve to sleep at night.

How We Can Really Learn From Animals

Animals can help doctors save human patients. But through observation – not experimentation. Many vertebrates – including monkeys, pigs and elephants, use plants as medicines as well as food. Sick animals seek out and eat plants which they know will help them; they eat some plants, they hold others in their mouths (doctors call it buccal absorption) and they rub yet others onto their skin (doctors call that topical application).

Ethiopian baboons who are at risk of developing schistosomiasis eat fruits which are rich in a potent antischistosome drug. Chimpanzees in Tanzania use a herb which has a powerful antifungal, antibacterial and antinematode activity. If they just ate the herb it wouldn't work because the valuable compound would be destroyed by stomach acidity. So they hold the leaf in their mouths in the same way that angina patients are encouraged to hold glyceryl trinitrate in their mouths to expedite absorption. Kodiak bears apply a drug topically which helps to kill parasites. They scratch the root into their fur. European starlings combat parasitisation in their nests by fumigating incubating eggs. Lethargic chimps with diarrhoea treat themselves with a herb. Howler monkeys use herbal medicines to control birth spacing and to determine the sex of their offspring.

We can learn an enormous amount by watching other animals.

But instead of watching these sensitive, intelligent and thoughtful creatures the vandals in white coats cage them, torture them and kill them with all the scientific sense of youthful hooligans tearing the wings off butterflies.

In a generation or so our descendants will, I hope and pray, look back at the vivisectors and wonder not just at the sort of people they were, but at the sort of people we were to let them do what they did.

Animal experiments must stop. And they must stop now. For your sake; for your children's sake; and for the sake of the animals the vivisectors kill.

Just For Fun

Human beings also abuse animals for fun.

We complain about bear baiting in Asia and about bull fighting in Spain. But we are in no position to condemn. In Britain people put on fancy dress and ride around chasing foxes, stags and other animals to their death. They do this primarily as entertainment but claim that they are trying to preserve the countryside.

If challenged and threatened with an end to hunting they sulkily threaten to kill their horses and hounds if their fun is stopped. They don't even have the courage to admit that they are merely blood thirsty psychopaths who get a kick out of killing.

Hunting continued into the twenty first century in Britain because it was preserved by a Labour government, despite the fact that the people and parliament opposed this barbaric remnant of our infant civilisation. A year after it dramatically refused to help a private members bill to ban hunting (in November 1997) the Labour government blocked any prospect at all of a ban on hunting being introduced into parliament. It was reported that the government (the same Labour government which had, when in opposition, stated its total commitment to banning hunting) feared that outlawing hunting would damage Labour's popularity in rural areas. When a government betrays the voters who put it into power, and ignores the wishes of the people, it effectively disenfranchises the electorate, leaving them with no say over their own destiny. Where then is democracy?

The stag or the fox being chased by a pack of yapping hounds and a bunch of ignorant rural yahoos on horseback is just as terrified as you would be if you were being chased by a gang of bloodthirsty hooligans on motorbikes.

Hunters (whether they hunt with a gun or on horseback) and hunt supporters are, without exception, wicked and barbaric people. When two men on a drunken hunting trip failed to find any deer they cold bloodedly murdered a deaf, black man instead. Typical and probably 'normal' behaviour for a hunter.

J. Howard Moore tells a sad story about two moose in his classic book *The Universal Kinship*. The two moose had been tracked by hunters all day long and towards the end of the day one of the moose was finally killed by a rifle shot. Instead of running away, the remaining moose lowered its head and sniffed at its dead companion. It then raised its head high and bellowed loudly. The ruthless hunters shot it. When the hunters reached the two moose they found that the one they had shot first had been blind and that the second moose, which had stayed with it even after death, had been acting as its pilot.

Waterfowl mate for life but human beings randomly shoot one and leave the other to mourn. The waterfowl which is left behind often falls into a deep depression. It may die slowly of starvation.

Hunters and their supporters are the sort of people who used to run the slavery trade just a few score years ago; they are not a sensitive group and they find it difficult to understand words such as 'empathy' and 'respect'. Hunters are pretty stupid and most of them aren't very good shots either. French hunters shot 45 of their fellow hunters dead in one recent season. More than 100 hunters were seriously injured by other hunters.

A Dirty Fight

The last few years of the fight for animal rights is going to be a dirty fight. Those who want to continue abusing animals – whether for money or for fun – fight foul.

Although my campaigning on behalf of animals and people has always been entirely legal I have been followed by private detectives, my life has been threatened and my telephone has been tapped by those who want to silence me. I have, of course, also been subjected to a considerable amount of legal harassment. In my experience supporting animal rights seems to attract a particularly virulent type of opposition – partly, I suspect, because this is the last great moral debate of our times (and many people feel guilty and slightly uncomfortable about the side they have chosen to support) and partly because the commercial forces which are dependant upon continuing animal abuse are large and powerful.

I do not approve of or support the use of violence in the fight against cruelty to animals. I do not approve of the use of violence against animal abusers. When you fight against violence with violence you simply double the amount of violence. But I do think that it is curious to note that when South African civil rights leaders used violence in their fight for justice and equality they were regarded as folk heroes and greeted with adoration by those who undoubtedly regard themselves as free thinking radicals. But whenever animal rights protestors have indicated a willingness to take relatively modest action against property in their fight against animal abuse they have aroused almost unrelieved opposition from those same self-styled, free-thinking radicals. It seems that the rules vary according to the battle being fought. The battle against apartheid threatened virtually no institutions outside South Africa but the battle against animal abuse threatens numerous large, profitable institutions. Many of Britain's self styled free thinking radicals are, it seems, more closely allied to the needs of the establishment (and the controlling institutions) than they might like us to think. Left wing pseudointellectuals and their broadsheet champions are not quite as left wing or as intellectual as they like to think they are.

There are going to be some surprising and unexpected casualties in the last great civil rights battle. It isn't just the pseudointellectual regiments of the false left who going to have to face some unpleasant truths as the battle against animal cruelty continues. Many other groups are going to suffer too.

For example, official Catholic teaching is that animals are here for man to use in any way he sees fit: to eat, kill for fun or play around with in the laboratory. Many Catholics believe that it is a sin to show affection to animals. Jews kill animals for food in the most barbaric way imaginable. And sanctimonious Christians frequently inform me that it is perfectly all right to treat animals in any way we wish because they don't have souls. Some exponents of the Christian religion teach that non-human races have no reason for their existence other than to serve man. They offer no evidence to support this arrogant and outrageous suggestion.

Tragically, too many citizens who might have the potential to care pretend that none of this is happening. They close their eyes, partly because they are ignorant of the truth about the way animals are abused, partly because they are still subject to long established prejudices in favour of human beings, partly because they are frightened (the animal abusers are rough, ruthless and powerful people with a lot of money to spend on preserving their power) and partly because they do not believe that anything they do can possibly change the way things are.

Complacent And Sanctimonious

I met a stranger recently who was, so he told me, a religious man. He had an aura of complacent, sanctimonious superiority. He asked me why I spent so much of my life fighting battles and trying to change the world. "Why, for example, do you put so much effort into trying to stop animal experiments?"

"I want to stop the cruelty," I told him.

"Ah!" he said, smiling and pointing a finger at me. "But what is cruelty?"

I stared at him for a moment. I had not thought the concept in need of clarification. I thought of Gertrude Stein. Cruelty is cruelty is cruelty is cruelty.

"Unjustified violence causing unnecessary pain," I suggested. "If someone pours a toxic chemical into the brain of a conscious cat I would call that cruelty."

"But the act of cruelty may be an act of kindness. How do you know that goodness does not come out of those experiments which you abhor?" he demanded.

"Even if good did come out of them – which it does not – I would not consider them justifiable," I said.

He leant forward across the table and smiled. "Isn't this enjoyable?" he said. "I do find debate so invigorating, don't you?"

I sat on my hands. "If one experiment on one rat could banish all human diseases it would not be justified," I told him.

"Oh," he said, clearly surprised.

"If you support animal experimentation then where do you draw the line? A cat is more intelligent than a baby. Do you support experimentation on babies? What about the elderly? The insane? Do you think that Mengele's work was justified?"

"Ah, now that is unfair," he said, suddenly rather put out. But still he smiled. I began to feel that he was a man in whose vocabulary passion did not figure largely. I found him loathsome, contemptible and vapid but there was nothing there to hate. He was that most nauseating of creatures: a not very bright pseudo-intellectual.

"The world must be allowed to change at its own pace," he said. "Over thousands of years if necessary. That is the only type of change that will last."

I stared at him. "But slavery was abolished through protest," I argued.

"Ah," he said. "But has anything really changed? Are not today's citizens just as much in bondage as those slaves of yesterday?"

"Women have the vote and apartheid has been smashed," I pointed out, numbed by the temerity of a man who could equate the slavery of the clock, the daily bus and the monthly wage packet to the slavery of the whip and outright ownership. I rather fancied that the man at the end of the whip would swap his bloody scars for the right to choose a seat on the 8.15 to Paddington. "Change came about because people protested," I said.

He shook his head. "I suspect that these changes would have eventually occurred without all the fuss and shouting." He smiled smugly. "The only true way to improve the world is to encourage each individual to become a better person," he said. "Otherwise when you banish one evil another will come in its place."

"But if you say nothing there will always be evil!" I protested. "Even if 99% of the population become good the 1% of psychopaths who are left will disrupt and destroy and spread evil."

"Then we must wait until they too are turned to goodness," he replied.

This was clearly a man of apparently unending patience where the pain and suffering of other creatures was concerned. I stared out of the window; frustrated, angry and saddened by this man's deep callousness and the extraordinary extent of his self delusion. I felt sickened by his comfortable, patronising smugness; nauseated by his unquestioning, uncaring, unseeing mediocrity. No vision, no passion, no love. He seemed full of self satisfaction and he exuded complacency.

"Of course," he said, "I do concede that you may be partly right in what you say about animal experiments."

"But if you concede that I am partly right," I said, "don't you want to do anything to right the wrong that exists? If one lamb, one puppy, one kitten, one mouse is treated cruelly do you not feel an urge to do something?"

He looked at me without comprehension. His eyes were empty of true understanding or compassion. A religious man but a man without a soul. I knew he did not understand. I felt then, and still feel, almost suffocated by sadness; a great universal sadness. I am no biblical scholar but I found myself remembering the scene where Jesus Christ walks into a church and finds it packed with money lenders and merchants (probably selling the early equivalent of postcards, slide sets, videos and souvenir ashtrays). Christ loses his temper, pushes over all the tables and throws out the money lenders and the merchants.

My sadness is that there are millions like that stranger; he is no rarity in this world. They are driven by a philosophy of avoidance. Avoid responsibility. Avoid conflict. Avoid action. Cross over the road to avoid the blood, the embarrassment or the involvement. I seem to remember that in the story of the good samaritan it was the religious man who crossed to the other side of the road and ignored the stranger in need. Too often, those who claim to have strong religious principles do not seem to be driven to fight very hard (if at all) for the downtrodden and the underprivileged.

Ignorance can be forgiven but wilful avoidance cannot. Those who neatly sidestep responsibility and produce pseudo-intellectual arguments designed to justify their silence in the face of injustice can never be forgiven. Those who go through life blinkered to injustice and to the pain and suffering of others condone cruelty. It is their silence which allows cruelty.

I like animals. And so does my God.

Part Two

Excuses, Excuses

Chapter One

They Claim That Animals Are Not Sentient Creatures

There is really only one underlying reason for animal abuse. The bottom line, is a five letter word beginning with M and ending in Y.

But animal abusers have, over the years, offered an almost endless series of well rehearsed, oft-repeated pseudo-arguments to excuse their barbaric behaviour. These excuses have been frequently used to help a modern Labour government which must, at times, have come perilously close to shame and embarrassment.

For example, those who abuse animals frequently claim that animals do not need or deserve special treatment because they are not 'sentient' creatures – in other words that they are not conscious creatures with the capacity to suffer and/or experience enjoyment or happiness.

A similar argument was used by those who supported slavery. The slavery proponents argued that Negroes did not blush because they were incapable of shame and were, therefore, not fully human. Interestingly a number of animals and birds have been observed to blush when excited (and do, therefore, satisfy these traditional requirements for 'human' behaviour). The Tasmanian devil, the turkey, macaws and monkeys are among the creatures known to blush. (Macaws, for example, have been reported to blush when accidentally falling while clambering down off a perch.)

It was also argued that black people were not capable of looking after themselves or their own interests because they were irrational. This was regarded as a good excuse for keeping black people in 'protective custody', and for exposing them to unlimited abuse.

Animal abusers are similarly inventive (but shallow) when attempting to excuse their cruel behaviour. Showing an extraordinary level of inconsistency and intellectual emptiness supporters of animal abuse have claimed, when defending fox hunting, that although animals are not sentient and have no feelings they 'enjoy' being hunted. It is difficult to see how anyone can possibly hope to sustain the argument that animals who are not sentient can 'enjoy' anything, but the supporters of animal abuse are full of contradictions, double-speak and self-deceit. People who deny that animals can suffer will also claim that animals can be cruel. (How can an animal be cruel if the animal to which it is supposed to be cruel cannot suffer?)

Ignorance And Abuse

The intellectual abuse and slander of animals has had an effect. Many people now don't care a damn about animals because they do not think of them as sentient creatures. It is this ignorance which is partly to blame for the fact that the cruel and abusive are allowed to continue to be cruel and abusive.

Sitting in a pub one day I couldn't help overhearing a telling conversation at the next table. A woman told her quite respectable looking companions how a friend of hers, a laboratory scientist experimenting on animals, had got fed up with anaesthetizing the rats he was using. And so, she said, instead of giving them a chemical anaesthetic he used to swing them around by their tails and knock them out by banging their heads on the workbench. She illustrated this hideous manoeuvre several times with a slick hand motion. She and her companions then laughed heartily. If a teenage thug had been spotted doing this he would have been taken to court. But I believe that this sort of thing is a regular occurrence in laboratories, which are almost exclusively populated by sickening and barbaric psychopaths. I still find it frightening that the woman in the pub, and her mindless companions, thought the evil actions of this vivisector were simply funny. But it is that sort of mindless approval of what goes on in laboratories that ensures that nothing changes and that animals continue to be abused.

Animals Have Moods And Feelings

Surely, anyone with an even modest intellect and a capacity to observe should know that animals have moods and feelings just the same as human beings do? And why shouldn't they? Why should human beings be so unique in that regard? There is surely something odd and illogical – although undoubtedly convenient for their purposes – about animal abusers assuming that animals and people are similar enough in anatomical and physiological terms for vivisection experiments to be of value but, at the same time, assuming that animals have no emotions. But then there is something odd and illogical about most things that the animal abusers do.

The available scientific evidence proves that although animals are very different to human beings in physiological and anatomical terms (so different as to make vivisection experiments worthless) animals show a similar range of intellectual skills and emotions to human beings.

They are not the same intellectual skills and emotions but that doesn't make them invalid. Animals do not recognise one another by name or clothing (as we often do). But they can recognise one another by smell, by sound and by instinctive skills which we either do not possess or have lost through not using them.

Animals Are Sentient

The truth, as anyone who is capable of reading and observing will know, is that animals are not only sentient but also exhibit many of those qualities which racists like to think of as being the preserve of the human race. (I think it is perfectly fair to describe those who claim that all 'good' qualities are the exclusive property of the human species as exhibiting a form of racism. The word 'speciesism' is, it seems to me, accurate but rather clumsy. We talk about the 'human race' and so, presumably, acknowledge that there are other 'non-human races'.)

One of the absurdities of the discussion about hunting which has raged for recent years in Britain has been the sight of apparently intelligent people arguing about whether or not animals which are hunted suffer physical pain and/or mental anguish when they are being pursued to the death. How can there possibly be any debate? Those who do express doubt about this are telling us a great deal about their own innate lack of understanding and compassion, and their inability to learn from simple observation. If observation is not enough there is more than enough scientific evidence to show that birds, mammals, fish, reptiles and crustaceans all have nervous systems and all suffer pain.

Darwin showed that fear produces similar responses in both humans and animals. The eyes and mouth open, the heart beats rapidly, teeth chatter, muscles tremble, hairs stand on end and so on. Parrots, like human beings, turn away and cover their eyes when confronted with a sight which overwhelms them. Young elephants who have seen their families killed by poachers wake up screaming in the night. Elephants who are suddenly separated from their social group may die suddenly of 'broken heart syndrome'. Apes may fall down and faint when suddenly coming across a snake. If a man shouts at a dog the animal may cower and back away in fear.

Animals Can Communicate

Animal abusers sometimes assume that it is only humans who can communicate with one another. This is total nonsense. Even bees can communicate. They can tell one another the direction, distance and value of pollen sources quite a distance away.

Animal abusers generally dismiss animal noises as simply that (noises) but scientists who have taken the time and trouble to listen carefully to the extraordinary variety of noises made by whales have found that there are patterns of what can only be described as speech which are repeated from one year to another.

It is generally assumed that parrots merely repeat words they have heard without understanding what they mean. This is not true. Masson and McCarthy report how when a woman left her parrot at the vet's surgery for an operation the parrot, whose name was Alex, called out: "Come here. I love you. I'm sorry. I want to go back." The parrot clearly thought that he was being punished for some crime he had committed. Another parrot, in New Jersey, US saved the life of its 'owner' by calling for help. "Murder! Help! Come quick!" cried the parrot. When neighbours ran to the scene of the crime they found the parrot's 'owner' lying on the floor, unconscious, bleeding from a gash in his neck. The doctor who treated the man said that without the parrot's cries he would have died. The same parrot woke his owner and neighbours when a fire started in the house next door.

How arrogant the animal abusers are to assume that human beings are the only species capable of communicating with one another, and of formulating a formal system of language.

Vivisectors frequently laugh at the animals they torture and abuse. The concentration camp guards in the second world war laughed at their victims and called them lice and rats. The vivisectors talk about 'sending a mouse to college' when they want to raise funds for experiments.

We have the power to do what we will with creatures of other species. But no one has given us the right to abuse our power. Civilised people respect, rather than abuse, the power they are given.

Animals feel complex emotions. But the animal abusers claim that because animals do not satisfy our human criteria for intelligence animals do not deserve any sympathy or understanding. It is but one step from this to arguing that unintelligent humans can be used for experiments, eaten or abused in any other selected way.

Human beings who have taken the time and trouble to do so have found that they have been able to communicate well with chimpanzees and numerous other animals. It is known that monkeys can grasp the concept of numbers and can learn to count. Primates will often strive to make the peace after a hostile encounter. Uninvolved primates may help begin and cement the reconciliation. And yet vivisectors are given legal licences allowing them to do horrific things to these animals. Who gave human beings the right to hand out licences to torture?

Capable Of Love

Animals, like people, are capable of loving their partner, their families, their children, their leaders, their teachers, their friends and others who are important to them. An ape will show exactly the same signs of love and affection when dealing with her baby as a human mother will when dealing with hers. Both will look longingly, tickle and play with their baby. Both feed their young, wash them, risk their lives for them and put up with their noise and unruly behaviour.

Anyone who doubts that animals love their young should stand outside a farm yard when a calf has been taken away from a cow and listen to the heart breaking cries of anguish which result. Who knows what inner anguish accompanies those cries?

Even fish will risk their lives to protect their young. In his seminal work *The Universal Kinship* (first published in 1906 and now largely forgotten) J. Howard Moore described how he put his hand into a pond near the nest of a perch. The courageous fish guarding the nest chased Moore's hand away and when Moore's hand was not removed quickly enough nipped it vigorously.

Lewis Gompertz, who lived from 1779 to 1861 and was a potent champion of the rights of blacks, women and the poor (and, indeed, all oppressed human beings) was also a powerful champion of animals and was a founder of the Royal Society for the Prevention of Cruelty to Animals. (Quite early on he was forced out of the Society.) In his book *Moral Inquiries On the Situation Of Man And Of Brutes* Gompertz wrote: "From some birds we may learn real constancy in conjugal affection, though in most instances their contracts only last for one season, but how strict do they keep this. They have no laws, no parchments, no parsons, no fear to injuring their characters, not even their own words to break in being untrue to each other: but their virtue is their laws, their parchments, their parsons, and their reputation; their deeds are their acts, their acts – their deeds: and from their own breasts do they honestly tear down to line the beds of their legitimate offspring."

Gompertz described an incident illustrating the wisdom of blackbirds. "I observed a male blackbird flying about in an extreme state of agitation," he wrote. "And on my going to discover the cause of it, the bird retreated from me as I followed it, till it stopped at a nest containing a female bird sitting upon her eggs, near which there was a cat: in consequence of this I removed the cat, and the bird became quiet. After that, whenever the cat was about the place, the blackbird would come near my window, and would in the same manner direct me to some spot where the cat happened to be stationed."

Gompertz, who also wrote about a male blackbird which had attacked a cat which had caught its female partner, reported three true incidents which illustrated animal kindness or wisdom.

The first concerned two goats which had met one another on a narrow path between two precipices. There was no room for the two goats to turn or pass and so one of the goats lay down, allowing the other to walk over it. The second incident involved a horse who had been hurt by a nail when he had been shod. Finding it painful to walk he had gone back to the farrier and shown him his hoof. The third incident involved a sheep dog who jumped into freezing cold water and successfully rescued another dog who had been floating on a lump of ice. "I would now fain ask," wrote Gompertz, "if all this does not show reason and virtue?"

J. Howard Moore described how monkeys adopt the orphans of deceased members of their tribe and how two crows fed a third crow which had been wounded. The wound was several weeks old and the two crows had clearly been playing 'good Samaritans' for some time to keep the injured bird alive.

Darwin wrote about a blind pelican which was fed with fish which were brought to it by pelican friends who normally lived thirty miles away.

Strong males in a herd of vicunas will lag behind to protect the weaker and slower members of their herd from possible predators.

Before slavery was abolished black people who fell in love were regarded as enjoying simple 'animal lust' as a result of 'animal attraction'. Who on earth (or, indeed, in heaven) gave us the right to make such judgements about black people or animals? When black people formed life long pairs this was dismissed as nothing more than a response to an 'instinct'. The same thing is said about animals (with just as little evidence to support it). Who gives humans the right to argue that animals do not show emotions? Animal abusers sneer and say that animals who seem to show love are merely acting according to instinct. But who says? Where is the evidence for this claim? Why do animal abusers have the right to make statements with no evidence whatsoever in support? Why don't the animal abusers follow a consistent line and argue that human mothers who show love for their human babies are merely following their instincts? (Of course, animal abusers change their views when it suits them. Even vivisectors and hunters, who claim that animals have no feelings, will often claim to be loved by their companion dogs and cats.)

There are numerous, well-authenticated stories of animals risking their lives to save their loved ones. And animals will put their own safety second to protect their friends. One herd of elephants was seen always to travel unusually slowly. Observers noted that the herd travelled slowly so as not to leave behind an elephant who had not fully recovered from a broken leg. Another herd travelled slowly to accommodate a mother who was carrying her dead calf with her. When the herd stopped to eat or drink the mother would put her dead calf down. When they started travelling she would pick up the dead calf. The rest of the herd were accommodating her in her time of grief. Gorillas too have been seen to travel slowly if one of their number is injured and unable to move quickly. Remember this unquestioning generosity next time you are trapped in the midst of a crowd of selfish and impatient human beings travelling by car, train or aeroplane.

Powerful Memories

Many creatures have memories which humans might envy. Ants retrace their steps after long journeys and can recognise other ants after months of separation. When a limpet has finished roaming it will return to the exact spot on the same rock where it had been settled previously. Birds fly back year after year to the same nesting spots – to within the inch. Fish return to the same stretch of water to hatch their young. Horses used in delivery routes frequently know exactly where and when to stop – and for how long. Squirrels who have buried nuts months before can find them without hesitating.

J. Howard Moore reported that an elephant obeyed all his old words of command on being recaptured after fifteen years of freedom in the jungle. He also reported that a lion recognised its keeper after seven years of separation. A snake which was carried a hundred miles away from home managed to find its way back.

There is plenty of evidence, too, to show that many creatures other than human beings have powerful imaginations. Spiders will hold down the edges of their webs with stones to steady them during gales which have not yet started. Cats, dogs and horses and many other creatures are believed to dream. Parrots may talk in their sleep. Horses frequently stampede because they are frightened by objects (such as large rocks or posts) which are no threat to them. This must show a sense of imagination because the horse, like a child, has created a terror out of nothing. A cat playing with a ball of wool is imagining that it is playing with its prey.

We always tend to think the worst of animals (and other creatures). We assume that they are stupid and our interpretation of their behaviour is based upon that ill founded prejudice. It is, for example, generally assumed that the ostrich sticks its head in the sand in the assumption that when it cannot see the rest of the world, the rest of the world cannot see it. But where is the evidence for this theory? Could it not be equally possible that the ostrich sticks its head in the sand because it cannot bear what there is to view in the world around it? When a human being covers his or her eyes to avoid looking at a horrific accident we do not say that they believe that they can't be seen.

Altruistic Behaviour

Animals don't just show love; they frequently exhibit behaviour that can only be described as altruistic. Old lionesses who have lost their teeth and can no longer bear young are, theoretically, of no value to the rest of the pride. But the younger lions will share their kills with them. Young, agile chimpanzees will climb trees to fetch fruit for their older relatives. Foxes have been observed bringing food to adult, injured foxes. When one fox was injured by a mowing machine and taken to a vet by a human observer the fox's sister took food to the spot where the injured fox had lain. The good Samaritan sister fox made the whimpering sound that foxes use when summoning cubs to eat (even though she had no cubs).

Animals have been known to give food to hungry humans. Koko, a gorilla who learned to communicate with humans through sign language, gave medical advice to a human woman who complained of indigestion. Koko told the woman to drink orange juice. When the human revisited ten days later and offered Koko a drink of orange juice Koko would not accept the drink until assured that the woman felt better. Whales have been observed to ask for and receive help from other whales. J. Howard Moore describes how crabs struggled for some time to turn over another crustacean which had fallen onto its back. When the crabs couldn't manage by themselves they went and fetched two other crabs to help them.

A gander who acted as a guardian to his blind partner would take her neck gently in his mouth and lead her to the water when she wanted to swim. Afterwards he would lead her home in the same manner. When goslings were hatched the gander, realising that the mother would not be able to cope, looked after them himself. Pigs will rush to defend one of their number who is being attacked. When wild geese are feeding one will act as sentinel – never taking a grain of corn while on duty. When the sentinel geese has been on watch for a while it pecks at a nearby goose and hands over the responsibility for guarding the group. When swans dive there is usually one which stays above the water to watch out for danger.

Time and time again dogs have pined and died on being separated from their masters or mistresses. Animals can suffer, they can communicate and they can care. A Border collie woke a young mother from a deep sleep and led her to her baby's cot. The baby was choking on mucus and had stopped breathing. What is any of this but compassion? How can animal abusers regard themselves as sentient when they mistreat animals who can feel this way?

Konrad Lorenz described the behaviour of a gander called Ado when his mate Susanne-Elisabeth was killed by a fox. Ado stood by Susanne-Elisabeth's body in mourning. He hung his head and his body was hunched. He didn't bother to defend himself when attacked by strange geese. How would the animal abusers describe such behaviour other than as sorrow born of love? There is no survival value in mourning. It can only be a manifestation of a clear emotional response – love.

A badger was seen to drag another badger which had been killed by a car off the road, along a hedge, through a gap in the hedge and into a burial spot in nearby woods.

Coyotes form pairs before they become sexually active – and then stay together. One observer watched a female coyote licking her partner's face after they had made love. They then curled up and went to sleep. Geese, swans and mandarin ducks have all been described as enjoying long term relationships.

Vanity And Self-Consciousness

Animals have also been known to show vanity, self consciousness, embarrassment and other allegedly exclusively human emotions. Masson and McCarthy reported that chimpanzees have been observed using a TV video monitor to watch themselves make faces – the chimpanzees were able to distinguish between a live image and taped image by testing to see if their actions were duplicated on the screen. Chimpanzees have even managed to use a video monitor to apply make up to themselves (humans often find this a difficult trick to learn). One chimpanzee has been reported to have used a video camera and monitor to look down his throat – using a flashlight to help the process.

As for vanity: "...males (baboons) with worn or broken teeth yawn less than male baboons with teeth in good condition – unless there are no other males around in which case they yawn just as often," write Masson and McCarthy.

One gorilla who had a number of toy dolls used sign language to send kisses to her favourite puppets and dolls. But every time she realised that she was being watched she stopped playing.

When a bottlenose porpoise accidentally bit her trainer's hand she became 'hideously embarrassed', went to the bottom of her tank, with her snout in a corner, and wouldn't come out until the trainer made it clear that she wasn't cross.

Jane Goodall has reported that wild chimpanzees can show embarrassment and shame and may also show off to other animals whom they want to impress. (One chimpanzee who fell while showing off was clearly embarrassed.)

Many people who live with cats will have noticed that if the cat falls off a piece of furniture it will appear embarrassed – often beginning to wash itself as though making it clear that the embarrassing incident didn't really happen at all. Elephant keepers report that when elephants are laughed at they will respond by filling their trunks with water and spraying the mockers. And many dog owners have reported that their animals have made it clear that they know when they have done wrong. For example a dog which feels it has done something wrong may go into a submissive position before the owner knows that the animal has done something 'bad'.

Artistic Animals

There are many myths about animals and the animal abusers tell many lies in an attempt to belittle the skills that animals have. It is, for example, sometimes said by animal abusers that sheep are stupid. This is a nonsense. Four sheep who lived with me, who were accustomed to being fed from an orange bucket, would come running across a field if they saw the orange bucket. When I used a blue bucket they showed absolutely no interest. The colour was the only significant difference between the buckets.

A chimpanzee has been observed staring at a beautiful sunset for fifteen minutes. Monkeys prefer looking at pictures of monkeys to pictures of people and prefer looking at animated cartoons rather than at still pictures.

Gerald Durrell wrote about a pigeon who listened quietly to most music but who would stamp backwards and forwards when marches were being played and would twist and bow, cooing softly, when waltzes were played. Dogs will alter their howling according to the other sounds they hear. One gorilla enjoyed the singing of Luciano Pavarotti so much that he would refuse to go out of doors when a Pavarotti concert was being shown on television. Animal abusers have for years dismissed bird song as merely mating calls. But who can say that birds do not sing to give themselves and others pleasure? Animals get pleasure from their food too. An Indian elephant in a zoo used to split an apple into two and then rub the two halves onto hay to flavour it.

Many apes have painted or drawn identifiable objects while in captivity. And when a young Indian elephant was reported to have made numerous drawings (which were highly commended by artists who did not know that the artist was an animal) other zoo keepers reported that their elephants often scribbled on the ground with sticks or stones. When one Asian elephant got extra attention because of her paintings nearby African elephants used the ends of logs to draw on the walls of their enclosure. (I do not approve of keeping animals in zoos but these simple observations are of value.)

The animal abusers invariably try to think the worst when considering animal behaviour. When a bird takes bright objects to decorate its nest the animal abusers will claim that the bird doesn't really know what it is doing. When a human being collects bird feathers to decorate a room they are said to be showing artistic tendencies.

Vivisectors, and others who abuse animals, are blind to all this because they want to be blind to it. Animal abuse is driven by economic need and there is no place for sentiment and compassion when money is at stake. Vivisectors tear animals away from their partners, their friends and their relatives with no regard for their feelings – or for the feelings of the animals they have left behind. Animals in captivity often die far younger than they would die if they were allowed to roam free.

When animals are born in zoos the keepers and jailers claim that this is evidence that the animals are happy. Would they also claim that the fact that babies were born in concentration camps is evidence that concentration camp inmates were happy?

What trickery the animal abusers use in their sordid attempts to excuse their brutality.

Smarter, Kinder, Better

Many other species – from families as varied as ants and dolphins – are smarter, kinder and better at creating societies which work than are human beings.

A survey showed that almost half of all the women in one US city had been raped, or subjected to attempted rape, at least once in their lives. Just think of the torture performed by humans on other humans.

Animal abusers will leap on every example they can find of apparent 'bad behaviour' by animals and use that example to draw far reaching conclusions about all animals. They ignore the fact that the 'bad behaviour' to which they refer may well have been triggered by human aggression.

Do the animal abusers who regard one example of bad animal behaviour as significant also suggest that because one human murders, tortures or rapes we must all be judged by that individual? Are all human beings to be judged to be as barbaric and evil as murderers, rapists and vivisectors?

As I have described in my book *Why Animal Experiments Must Stop* (published by the European Medical Journal) experimenters have deliberately planned and executed experiments designed to make animals feel depressed. When they have succeeded in making animals depressed they have written about their experiments as though proud of themselves for having succeeded in their evil aims. What possible purpose can there be in creating depression when there is already so much of it in the world? (But, incidentally, does not the ability of the experimental scientists to 'make' animals feel depressed provide yet more proof that animals are sentient creatures?)

Enjoying The Suffering

No animal, other than the human animal, has ever deliberately performed experiments on another. No one animal, other than the human animal, has ever deliberately tortured another being.

Human beings are the only species who abuse one another (and members of other species) for pleasure. Human beings are the only species who torture. Only human beings chase and attack living creatures for fun – and for the pleasure of watching the suffering.

Contrary to myth cats do not 'play' with animals for fun – it is part of their learning and training process. Cats kill so that they can eat and they need to practise their chasing skills. It is, however, important to remember that a cat or a kitten will be just as happy chasing a ball of paper or a piece of string (particularly if it is manipulated in an effective and lifelike manner). This shows that the cat doesn't chase and catch because it enjoys the suffering which is produced. How much 'fun' could there possibly be in 'torturing' a ball of paper or a piece of string?

Foxes are often criticised (by those who hunt them) on the grounds that they sometimes kill large numbers of hens. The implication is that the fox kills for pleasure. The truth, however, is that, like other predators who may kill more than they can eat when they have the opportunity, foxes store (or intend to store) the food they have killed.

Animals As Carers

In *When Elephants Weep* Jeffrey Masson and Susan McCarthy report how a man called John Teal, who was working with endangered musk oxen, was at first alarmed when some dogs approached and the musk oxen snorted, stamped and thundered towards him. Before John Teal could move to escape, the oxen formed a defensive ring around him and lowered their horns at the dogs. The musk oxen were protecting their new human friend in exactly the same way that they would protect their calves from predators.

Animals have even been reported to have pets of their own. A chimpanzee who was thought to be lonely was given a kitten as a companion. The chimpanzee groomed the kitten, carried it about with her and protected it from harm. A gorilla called Koko had a kitten companion which she herself named All Ball. An elephant was seen to routinely put aside some grain for a mouse to eat. Racehorses who have had goat companions have failed to run as expected when separated from their friends.

A Sense Of Fun

Human beings are not the only animals to have a sense of humour and fun and to enjoy playing.

Masson and McCarthy report that foxes will tease hyenas by going close to them and then running away. Ravens tease peregrine falcons by flying close and closer to them. Grebes tweak the tails of dignified swans and then dive to escape. I have watched lambs play their own version of 'King of the Castle' (and many other games customarily played by children). A monkey has been seen to pass his hand behind a second monkey so that he could tweak the tail of a third monkey. When the third monkey remonstrated with the second monkey the first monkey – the practical joker – clearly enjoyed himself.

When scientists examined the dung of lions, the lions (who had watched them do it) dug up the latrine the humans had been using – and inspected the contents. Ants, fish, birds, cats, dogs, sheep, horses, monkeys, porpoises and many other creatures often play games.

The Barbaric Abuse Of Sensitive Creatures

Animals frequently make friends across the species barriers. There is much evidence showing that animals have helped animals belonging to a different species. So, why do we have to be the only species to abuse all other creatures? Is our cruelty to other creatures really to be regarded as a sign of our wisdom, superiority and civilisation? What arrogance we show in the way we treat animals. Where is our humility and sense of respect?

Animals have passionate relationships with one another, they exhibit clear signs of love, they develop social lives which are every bit as complex as our own. By what right do we treat them with such contempt?

Perhaps those who torture and kill animals had to claim that animals have no feelings when they first started their evil practices (otherwise they would have had to admit that they themselves were acting cruelly) but how they can continue to do this when there is so much scientific evidence to prove that they are utterly wrong? I believe that some of those who torture and kill insist on being allowed to continue to torture and kill partly because they know that if they stop and admit that they were wrong to do what they did, they will have to admit that they have spent their lives in the senseless, unjustifiable and barbaric abuse of sensitive creatures.

No one with any intelligence or sensitivity of their own can possibly doubt that animals are capable of suffering. Animal experimenters, abattoir workers, hunters and others of that ilk degrade us all and diminish our worth as a species.

Better Than Animals?

The animal abusers will frequently argue that since human beings can speak foreign languages and do algebraic equations they are inevitably 'better' than animals. What nonsense this is. Does this mean that humans who cannot speak foreign languages or do algebraic equations are not entitled to be treated with respect? And who decides which are the skills deserving of respect? If it was decided that the ability to fly, run at 30 mph, see in the dark or swim under water for long distances were the skills worthy of respect there wouldn't be many human beings qualifying for respect.

Cats can find their way home – without map or compass – when abandoned hundreds of miles away in strange territory. How many human being could do the same? How many humans could spin a web or build a honeycomb?

We owe it to animals to treat them with respect and, at the very least, to leave them alone to live their lives on this earth free from our harm. Darwin wrote that: "there is no fundamental difference between man and the higher mammals in their mental faculties". He also argued that: "the senses and intuition, the various emotions and faculties, such as love, memory, attention, curiosity, imitation, reason etc. of which man boasts, may be found in an incipient, or sometimes even well-developed condition in the 'lower' animals."

Turtles have been observed learning a route from one place to another. To begin with they make lots of mistakes, go down cul-de-sacs and miss short-cuts. But after a while they learn how to reduce their journey time dramatically. Birds, who might normally be alarmed by the slightest noise, learn to ignore the noise of trains and cars when they build their nests near to railway lines or busy roads. Even oysters are capable of learning. Oysters who live in the deep sea know that they can open and shut their shells at any time without risk. But oysters who live in a tidal area learn to keep their shells closed when the tide is out – so that they don't dry out and die. This might not quite rank alongside writing a classic novel but how many human beings can write classic novels?

Animals use reason and experience to help them survive and they exhibit most of the skills which the animal abusers like to think of as being exclusively human.

Most people think of sheep as being pretty stupid animals. People who claim to have studied animal behaviour often argue that sheep do not have long term memories. But consider the following true story from when I had four sheep (Septimus, Karen, Cilla and Snowy) living with me.

One March I got my ride-on-mower out from the shed where it had been stored for the winter and started up the engine ready to drive it across the courtyard towards the garden. I intended to start by cutting the croquet lawn. As I started up the engine and the mower chugged slowly out of the shed I watched the four sheep, who were grazing in their field, prick up their ears and start to run. I watched as they ran for several hundred yards and then stood waiting at the very spot where, the previous summer, I had dumped the grass cuttings I had taken from the lawns.

It slowly dawned on me that the sheep had, after a gap of five or six months, recognised the sound of the lawn mower's engine (differentiating it from the numerous other engines they would have heard in the intervening period), recognised that the sound of the engine meant that I was about to start cutting the grass, remembered that they liked munching a handful of grass cuttings, remembered where I had dumped the grass cuttings some five or six months previously when I had last cut the lawns, and had instantly run round the field to be in position ready for the first batch of cuttings of the season.

Now all that seems to suggest to me that sheep are really very bright. I know a good many human beings (most of them politicians) who could not have used that one piece of information (the starting up of a lawnmower engine) and drawn such an accurate conclusion.

All animals accumulate information which helps them to survive and live more comfortably. Moreover, they do it just as man does – by discriminating between useful and useless information and by memorising information which is of value.

A puppy who has been burnt on a hot stove will keep away from the hot stove just as surely as a child who has suffered a similarly unpleasant experience. Older fish learn to be wary of lures – and become far more difficult to catch than young ones. Rats learn how to avoid traps, and birds learn where telephone wires are strung (so that they don't fly into them). Arctic seals used to live on inner ice floes to avoid the polar bears but after man arrived and proved to be a worse enemy they started living on the outer ice floes.

Many animals know that they can be followed by their scent and act accordingly. A hunted deer or hare will run round in circles, double back on its own tracks, go through water and leap into the air in order to lose its pursuers.

And flocks of parrots will send an advance scouting party ahead to check out that all is well.

To describe cruel people as 'animals' (something which the animal abusers often do) is a foul libel.

Animals As Teachers

There is no doubt, too, that animals actively teach their young in order to pass on skills which the animal abusers generally regard as being 'nothing more than instinct'. I have watched an adult cat giving lessons to orphan kittens for which he had taken responsibility. The adult cat, teaching the art of stalking, would edge forwards and then stop and look over his shoulder to see if the kittens were following in the correct style. After the lesson had gone on for some time the kittens started playing behind the adult cat's back. They got away with this for a while but eventually the adult cat saw them. He reached back and gave them both a clip with an outstretched paw. The kittens weren't hurt but they paid attention to their lesson again.

We tend to ignore the actions of other creatures because we don't have the time to watch what they do. But even the seemingly lowly ant has a complex and sophisticated life style. Ants can communicate with one another and they can recognise their friends. They clean one another, they play, they bury their dead, they store grain; they even clear land, manure it, sow grain and harvest the grass which they have grown.

When animal abusers hear about this sort of behaviour they dismiss at as nothing more than instinct. But is it? If a Martian looked down on earth and watched us rushing about on our routine daily work would he perhaps be tempted to describe us as incapable of original thought and responding only to instinct?

We may not like it but many races of non-human beings have a much greater influence on their environment than many men have. There are still tribes of men who live almost naked in very crude huts and whose social structures are relatively primitive when compared to, say, the beavers who cut down trees, transport them long distances, dam rivers, construct substantial homes and dig artificial waterways. Ants plant crops and build roads and tunnels. Birds build astonishingly beautiful nests from the simplest of materials.

Animal abusers claim that man is the only animal to use tools. But this simply isn't true. Even insects use tools – using small stones to pack the dirt firmly over and around their nests. As I've already pointed out, spiders use stones to keep their webs steady when the weather is stormy. Orangutans and baboons use sticks and stones as weapons. Monkeys use stones to help them crack nuts. In one zoo a monkey who had poor teeth kept (and guarded) a stone hidden in its straw for nut cracking. That monkey had a tool which it regarded as its own property. Chimpanzees drum on hollow logs with sticks. Monkeys know how to use sticks as levers. The Indian elephant will break off a leafy branch and use it to sweep away the flies.

Ants know how to keep grain in a warm, moist atmosphere without the grain sprouting. The honeycomb and the bird's nest are wonders of architecture. Insect communities practise true and decent socialism.

The wonders are unending.

Animals are often curious and determined and hard working; loving and loyal and faithful. (But they do not harm themselves with tobacco and alcohol.)

We do not understand how a cat which has been taken a hundred miles away from its home (in a closed bag) can find its way back again.

But animal abusers will sew up a cat's eyes, plant electrodes into its head and subject it to unimaginable pain and suffering in their search for financial, intellectual or personal reward.

The eagle and the vulture have eyes as powerful as a telescope. The swallow will travel thousands of miles every spring – only to be trapped and shot by a Maltese hunter when it dares to land to find fresh water.

Many animals, birds and insects can predict the coming of storms far more effectively than our allegedly scientific weather forecasters.

Weight for weight the tomtit has more brain capacity than a human being.

The animal abusers claim that animals cannot reason. But it is clear that it is the animal abusers who find reason a difficult concept.

The facts are abundantly clear: animals are sentient creatures. As J. Howard Moore put it: "The human species constitutes but one branch in the gigantic arbour of life."

How cruel and vicious a species we must look to lobsters who are boiled alive, to donkeys who are beaten beyond their endurance and to all farm animals.

Generally speaking, man is the most drunken, selfish, bloodthirsty, miserly, greedy, hypocritical being on the planet. And yet we think ourselves so damned superior. Man is the only being on the planet to kill for the sake of killing; to dress up and turn killing into a social pastime. It can truly be said that not all men are humane.

The animal abusers sneer at hyenas but they do not kill for fun. Only man gloats over the accumulation of material goods which he does not truly need. No creature is as immoral as the animal abuser. Only man needs an army of lawyers to fight over what is right and wrong. Only man has forgotten the meaning of natural justice.

We have created a hell on this earth for other creatures. Our abuse of animals is the final savagery, the final outrage of mankind in a long history of savagery and outrage. We have colonised other species in the same way that White Northern Europeans colonised other parts of the world. Instead of learning from other animals, instead of attempting to communicate with them, we simply thrash around wickedly, abusing, torturing, tormenting and killing. We destroy the relationships of animals with one another, with their environment and with our own race. We diminish ourselves in a hundred different ways through our cruelty and our ignorance and our thoughtlessness. "Man's inhumanity to man makes countless thousands mourn and his inhumanity to not-men makes the planet a ball of pain and terror," wrote J. Howard Moore.

If man was truly the master of the universe he would use his wisdom and his power to increase the comfort and happiness of all other sentient creatures. Sadly, tragically, man has used his wisdom and his power to increase the misery of other sentient creatures. Animal abusers imprison millions of animals in cruel and heartbreaking conditions and ignore their cries of pain and distress on the grounds that animals are not 'sentient creatures'. What self delusional nonsense this is.

Sheep and cattle are left out in huge fields in cold, wet weather. They shiver and search in vain for shelter because all the trees and hedgerows have been removed to make the farm more efficient. The animal abusing farmer cares not one jot for animals: he cares only for his profits.

It is quite simply just as immoral to regard animals as existing for the glorification of man as it is to regard black men or women as existing to serve white men.

"Until he extends the circle of his compassion to all living things," wrote Albert Schweizer, "man will not himself find peace."

The merciful man is kind to all creatures.

Chapter Two

They Claim That Animals Have No Souls And Take No Responsibility And Therefore Have No Rights

A few years ago I was invited to speak about animal issues in Johannesburg, South Africa. There was initially some difficulty in finding a supporter of animal abuse in general (and vivisection in particular) who was prepared to debate the issue with me in public. The only local academic who was prepared to defend his work in public agreed to do so on condition that the entire debate was conducted in Afrikaans. As he undoubtedly well knew, I do not speak Afrikaans.

Eventually, a speaker was flown in from somewhere else in South Africa to support the contention that scientists should be allowed to continue performing animal experiments. In the end science, the new savagery, must always be defended against the gentle campaigners at the citadel walls.

One of the main tenets of this speaker's argument was that since animals do not have souls they do not have rights. This is, of course, a point of view first put forward by René Descartes a long time ago. Descartes believed (with no evidence whatsoever to support the belief) that non-human animals lack souls, intelligence and the ability to feel pleasure, pain or, indeed, anything. According to Descartes if you hit an animal then it would cry out for just the same reason that a clock chimes or a bell rings. Despite his continuing reputation Descartes was clearly not a bright individual.

I recall rather angrily asking the woman in South Africa who had told her that animals do not have souls – and whether her god had confirmed this allegation. I seem to remember a lack of a clear response to this question.

The Intellectually And Morally Deprived

Bizarre though it may sound the primitive and self serving argument that animals have no souls is widely used by the intellectually and morally deprived.

The woman who goes to church on Sundays, wearing her fur coat with her hat adorned with feathers torn from birds, and who eats meat and hunts, undoubtedly thinks herself a godly and gentle woman when she mumbles prayers she does not understand and gives unearned pence for the building of ever more glorious churches.

Those who argue that animals have no souls usually add that animals are on this earth solely for the use of human beings and that it is, therefore, perfectly acceptable for us to do with them what we will.

This is, of course, exactly the same argument which was used in favour of slavery. "Negroes have no rights which the white man is bound to respect," a member of the US Supreme Court once said. (Ample proof, if proof be needed, that judges and the courts can and do make blunders of criminal proportions and may not always be capable of melding law with justice and moral rights.)

The attitude of the animal abusers towards other species should not be too much of a surprise to us. After all, every nation and, indeed, every tribe of human beings, has at some time or another looked down upon outsiders.

Some tribes in Africa used to punish theft within the tribe with death but encouraged and rewarded thieving from other tribes. In Afghanistan it was traditional for a woman to pray that her son would become a successful robber of strangers. The ancient Germans did not regard crimes committed beyond their boundaries as crimes at all. The Jews believed themselves to be superior to all other races, selected by their god to be above all others and given the right to make war upon the weak and to take their lands. The Greeks regarded all non-Greeks as barbarians and the Romans regarded all non-Romans as barbarians too. Romans kept slaves in abundance (they had so many slaves that a Roman would have one slave whose sole duty was to look after his master's sandals) but those slaves had no rights. The Chinese regarded their country as being the centre of the earth and the Spanish, the English, the French and the German have all regarded themselves as superior to the rest of the world. Even the US, a young nation with remarkably little to commend it other than size and wealth, has acquired an arrogant belief in itself as leader of the world.

The Christian looks down his nose at the Jew who looks down his nose at the Moslem who looks down his nose at the Christian.

An Easily Demolished Argument

A variation on the 'no soul – no rights' argument is to claim that animals do not, and can not, have any rights because they do not take any responsibility for their actions.

This must surely be one of the most easily demolished arguments in history and yet it is frequently repeated by people who obviously regard themselves as sentient and intelligent human beings. It is even used quite frequently in print and is consistently popular with pro-hunt supporters.

The fact is, of course, that this is a pseudo argument which can surely only have been thought up by, or be sustained by, the intellectually disadvantaged.

If not taking responsibility for one's actions denies one any rights then one must presume that the animal abusers would also be happy to deny rights to babies, the mentally ill, unconscious patients in hospital, the subnormal, patients suffering from disorders such as senile dementia and so on.

None of the people in these groups take responsibility for what they do. Does that mean that we are free to do with them what we will?

The animal abusers may have money, and they may have power, but they don't have much in the way of brains.

Social Structures

In fact, there is ample evidence that animals do often take a great deal of responsibility. They may not always show much responsibility towards human beings (or towards human values) but in that respect they are no different to human beings – who do not show much responsibility towards animals and animal values.

There is a great deal of evidence to show that animals have powerful social structures and even systems of justice. Animals who do wrong to other animals are punished and animals frequently make an effort to right injustices.

Our Duty

There is another point here which is rarely made by the animal abusers – who may not be sensitive enough or intelligent enough to have thought of it. If we, as human beings, are so astute, so clever, so sensitive and so superior is it not our responsibility to behave towards other species with kindness and respect?

Mischievous animal abusers will argue that people who insist on treating animals with respect must afford the same level of respect to all other living organisms. "If you want to be kind to animals," they will claim smugly, "then if a wasp wants to sting you you should let it."

They also try to force us to draw lines. If we are going to be kind to animals do we have to be kind to all animals or should we choose certain groups for preferential treatment? Should we be particularly kind to the primates? After all we are closer to the primates than we are to rabbits or snakes. Should we treat mammals with more respect than other creatures?

It is a common mistake to assume that Darwin regarded the human being as the finished product in the evolutionary process. Darwin actually wrote that: "animals may partake from our common origin in one ancestor...we may all be netted together".

He argued that humans and apes and orangutans are evolutionary first cousins. Darwin disapproved strongly of the attempt to use the philosophy of natural selection to excuse racism. (Racists have on many occasions argued that black people are members of a different species to white people.) Evolution, as described by Darwin, is a result of random genetic mutation. There is no sound moral basis for arguing that one mutation is better than another – or that the mutated version is inevitably better than the unmutated version. It may be different and have different attributes but that doesn't necessarily make it better.

The big answer, of course, is that this isn't our earth. We don't own it. We may have colonised it but we don't have the freehold. And we have a simple duty to treat all the other inhabitants with respect. We should not abuse or torture any living creature. There is no need for the drawing of lines between species which deserve our respect and species which don't. We should have respect for all other living creatures and we should not authorise or legalise cruelty. We should live our lives so as to cause as little pain as possible to other creatures (whether human or animal). We have no right to dominate any other creature. And although we do, of course, have the right to use whatever power is necessary to dissuade a wasp from stinging us there is no need for us to kill it to do this.

Any individual, of whatever species, who has the ability to suffer and to feel pain deserves to be treated with respect. We do not have the right to dominate any living creature or to despoil our environment. The abusers of animals abuse themselves too.

Arrant Nonsense

Those who abuse animals often argue that pro-animal campaigners do not care about people as much as animals. This is, of course, arrant nonsense. Just about everyone in history who has campaigned for people has also campaigned vigorously for animals. Abuse is abuse, whoever the victim may be. Abraham Lincoln, the 16th President of the US who abolished slavery, believed that animal rights were as important as human rights. William Wilberforce and Henry David Thoreau both fought for animals as well as people. Lord Shaftesbury, a social reformer who campaigned for free education and to stop children being employed in the mines campaigned against animal abuse and for the total abolition of vivisection. Albert Einstein was a vegetarian who fought for animal rights. John Locke, the philosopher, believed in animal rights as well as human rights and wrote that if children were cruel to animals it would harden their hearts towards other humans. Dr Albert Schweitzer, the theologian who won the 1952 Nobel Peace Prize, and is famed for his work in his African hospital was a vegetarian who believed in reverence for all forms of life. Leonardo Da Vinci was a vegetarian. Buddha, who founded the religion named after him, taught that men should not hurt or kill any living creature. Charles Darwin believed that to love all living creatures was the most noble attribute in man. C. S. Lewis and Robert Browning both campaigned against vivisection. Gandhi, who led the Indian people to independence by non violent means, was a vegetarian who believed that vivisection was the blackest of all the black crimes committed against god and his fair creation. Voltaire, the French author, attacked the absurd Cartèsian principle that animals were no more than machines. Mark Twain, the American humorist who supported many social reforms was a stern critic of all forms of animal abuse. Sir Isaac Newton believed that humanity should be extended to include animals. Jeremy Bentham, the philosopher and legal reformer believed that humanity should protect every creature which breathes. George Bernard Shaw, the Nobel Prize winning author and social reformer was a vegetarian who campaigned against all animal abuse including vivisection. The philosopher Arthur Schopenhauer wrote that "compassion for animals is intimately connected with goodness of character; and it may be confidently asserted that he who is cruel to animals cannot be a good man."

As a counterbalance to this short and by no means complete list of caring individuals a list of murderers who have also done unspeakable things to animals neatly proves the point that cruelty is cruelty and cruel people are cruel people.

Peter Kurten, known as the Dusseldorf Monster, murdered more than 50 people and practised bestiality on dogs as he tortured and killed them; Luke Woodham stabbed his mother and killed two teenage girls and also set fire to his own dog; David Berkowitz killed six people and also shot his neighbour's dog and poisoned his mother's parakeet; Patrick Sherrill who murdered 14 people stole local pets for his dog to attack; Jack Bassenti, a murderer and rapist buried puppies alive; Randy Roth killed two wives, and also used an industrial sander on a frog and taped a cat to a car engine; Edward Kemperer killed his grandparents, mother and seven other women and also chopped up cats; Henry Lee Lucas, who killed his mother and his wife also killed animals and had sex with their corpses; Michael Cartier, a murderer, threw a kitten through a closed window and pulled a rabbit's legs out of its sockets when he was four years old.

There is, it seems clear, a strong relationship between those who are cruel to animals and those who are cruel to humans. The sort of people who abuse animals (whether by experimenting on them, hunting them or hurting in some other way) are the same sort of people who abuse humans.

Surely we should be kind and considerate towards other creatures for exactly the same reason that we should be kind and considerate towards other human beings.

Why should we consider it a crime to torture a man to death – but support a government which gives public money to support a vivisector who tortures a monkey to death? Where is the justice or the logic in it? There is none.

If aliens landed on earth and started to treat us in the way that we now treat animals we would protest vehemently. What, pray, is the difference in the way we currently treat other living creatures?

"The love for all living creatures," wrote Charles Darwin, "is the most noble attribute of man." By that definition man is not a particularly noble creature.

As a final note it seems relevant to point out here that it is in any case impractical, if not impossible, to separate animal abuse from people abuse in the way that animal abusers try to do. Animal abuse and people abuse are inextricably and permanently linked. For example, the abuse of animals in the name of science, performed by vivisectors in laboratories, may appear to be solely an abuse of animals. But since the end result of such experiments is the production, marketing and prescribing of drugs which have not been adequately tested for human use people do suffer as a result of animal experiments. Similarly, the abuse of animals in the preparation of meat may not, at first, appear to involve much abuse of human beings. But since it is now known that eating meat is closely linked to the development of a number of types of deadly cancer those who are involved in killing animals for human consumption are also, inevitably, involved in killing human beings.

The farmer, the abattoir worker and the butcher who abuse animals in order to provide meat for the dining table are also directly responsible for the deaths of those people who have contracted cancer through eating meat.

Since those who work in the meat industry should know that the product they sell kills people it does not seem unreasonable to describe meat industry workers as murderers.

From A Human Standpoint

We look at everything from our unique, human standpoint. If a mouse wanders into an animal abuser's house and nibbles at a piece of cheese the animal abuser immediately puts down poison and sets traps all over the house. Animal abusers tear baby chimpanzees from their mothers, drag them thousands of miles, stick them into tiny cages and do unspeakable things to them in order to obtain academic status and glory.

J.Howard Moore tells a remarkable story in his book *The Universal Kinship*.

"One of the greatest obstacles missionaries have to contend with," wrote Moore, quoting from letters written by an American missionary in Burma, "is the hostility aroused in the people by the killing and flesh eating habits of the missionaries themselves. The native inhabitants, who are the most compassionate of mankind, look upon the Christian missionaries, who kill and eat cows and shoot monkeys for pastime, as being little better than cannibals. Contemplate the presumption necessary to cause an individual to leave behind him fields white for mission work, and travel, at great expense, halfway round the earth in order to preach a narrow, cruel, anthropocentric gospel to a people of so great tenderness and humanity as to be kind even to 'animals' and enemies!"

Anthropocentricism, a founding philosophy of Judaism, Christianity and Mahometanism, is an attitude of mind which has for centuries shaped the history of the world, and is undoubtedly the most conceited expression of human provincialism (and colonialism) ever devised.

According to this view of the world man is the centre of the universe – and of life itself. Everything else (including women and all other living creatures) is there for the pleasure of man.

If this were so one might reasonably assume that the several million non-human species on the planet earth would all be of value to mankind. But they aren't. Some species are a threat to man's life and survival as a species. Many are neither a help nor a hindrance. And what of the planets? What possible use are they to man?

Ancient man's assumption that the world was created for him should be a historical absurdity; but it isn't. This bizarre and obviously ill founded nonsense is still the basis for the widely held parochial conceit that animals, birds, fish and so on are all here solely for our delight.

Universal Kinship

The theory of the 'universal kinship' of man and other creatures, as taught by Buddha, Pythagoras and Plutarch has been pushed aside. Both Shelley and Tolstoy favoured universal kinship but few modern writers would dare to espouse themselves to such an out of favour philosophy.

The fact that not all creatures have equal rights does not, in the slightest, affect the principle that all creatures have rights. No one would argue that all men have equal rights (though many would argue that they should) but only a simple minded person would attempt to argue that inequality justifies taking away rights from some.

Some creatures fly, some make their home in the sea, some live for a day and some for a century or more. Some are brown, some are white, some are blue and some are green; some are tall and some are small. Some are wise and social, others are solitary and simple in thought. Some roam constantly while some are content to stay at home.

They are all tenants, and all entitled to share the glory of our earth.

Cruelty, Immorality And The Church

Malta is a noisy, squalid, smelly, god-forsaken, grubby little corner of Hell which seems to me to be populated by petty crooks and bloodthirsty, heathen barbarians whose idea of Sunday morning fun seems to be to play football with a kitten or blast a flight of swallows out of the sky with a shotgun.

There is virtually no birdsong on Malta. Apart from the raucous sound of an endless parade of intellectually deprived hooligans riding up and down the sea front playing out of date tapes of tuneless third rate kindergarten pop music on cheap, distorting car radios this wretched, miserable island is virtually silent. In a one week visit there I saw three nervous sparrows and a bunch of very stringy pigeons.

The violent, graceless, thieving barbarians who live on Malta have trapped or shot all the birds.

Have you ever wondered why, in autumn, we send off so many swallows and then, in spring, we get so few back? It is because the Maltese kill them. They kill anything that moves. They like killing. The bigger birds they stuff and sell. A few birds they eat. But the swallows – and millions of other birds – they kill for fun.

When God looks down on Malta he must weep. This is truly the island of the eternally damned. I have never been anywhere quite like Malta. Dishonesty is endemic. Cab drivers fiddle like a thousand Neros. The majority of the islanders seemed to me to be rude, sullen, ungracious and unwelcoming. Most of the resident, retired British expatriates seem to be suffering from a mixture of Alzheimer's Disease and Mad Cow Disease. They stumble along, dodging endless, moronic youths on roller skates and scuttle around looking for a half decent cup of tea, trekking from flat to shop and shop to flat in a pitiful daily ritual that mimics life.

But the squalor, the rudeness and the islanders' open determination to cheat the tourists of as much money as possible is, in a way, an irrelevance. What really disgusts me about this Mediterranean pustule is the way that animals are treated. Domestic cats, thrown out of their homes by bored Maltese or incontinent, retired British sunseekers, roam the streets in huge numbers. They rely entirely on the tourists for food.

Anyone who likes animals will find a day on Malta a sickening experience. Any sensitive being who loves animals will find the island – and its miserable inhabitants – unbearable.

In one week there I spent more on cat food than I did on food for myself. I wept with rage to see cats and other animals mistreated.

One morning I was shown half a dozen kittens being hidden in a dark hole in the wall. The kittens were let out into the sunlight for a few minutes each day. The person looking after them – who was asking for money from tourists to help buy food for fifty or sixty abandoned cats – had to hide the kittens away from Maltese youths. He knew that if the young Maltese found the kittens they would kill them for fun. They would either throw them into the sea and watch them drown or they would play football with them.

The following morning I saw another four kittens – abandoned in a cardboard box near to the sea. Whoever had dumped them had left them a pile of stale bread for food.

The Maltese do not seem to me to be normal people. As a nation they do not seem to have morals, souls and consciences. They claim to be Christian but no god would accept the hypocritical prayers of such evil people.

I spoke to several Maltese men who told me with pride that they regularly hunted birds and other creatures. They seemed proud to be killers.

The hunters use nets to catch the birds. They put a decoy bird into one net and then, when other birds fly down to help the trapped creature, they throw out a second net. When migrating birds set down on Malta to rest the hunters gleefully pounce. The innocent and unsuspecting are no match for the primitive cunning of these nasty little people.

When I remonstrated with one Maltese hunter he told me that if local politicians tried to stop the hunting they would be killed. He seemed proud of this.

I suspect that there is a lot of inbreeding on the island and it may be that many of the locals are a little simple. Their solitary skill is killing. And they specialise in killing the innocent and the defenceless.

When god created the Maltese he made a fundamental error. He packed their intestines with brain tissue and filled their skulls with the stuff that should have been inside their intestines.

When I wrote articles criticising the Maltese habit of slaughtering just about every living creature which dares to set paw, hoof or claw on their sad little Mediterranean island (and suggested that the next time the French wanted somewhere to test a bomb we should offer them Malta) there were inevitably many protests from the Maltese who felt aggrieved that I had exposed the truth about their island, and alarmed at the fact that as a result their tourist industry lay in tatters. I received a vast number of threatening letters – including one telling me that a 'hit' had been taken out on my life. (That response seemed to fit in well with the Maltese way of doing things.)

To be fair many people from the island agreed with me that something had to be done. Several were kind enough to write and say that my articles had done more than decades of local campaigning. I had it on good authority that the Maltese were making speedy plans to put a stop to some of the cruel practices which I had outlined.

But in my view, the oddest response came from someone who used my attack on Malta as an excuse for a lengthy response describing how committed the Maltese are to their local churches. Much to my surprise, at no point did this writer even mention the animals of Malta. The response praising the Maltese as church lovers contained not the merest mention of the way the Maltese treat animals.

It is my personal experience that many of the people who are enthusiastically involved with any sort of church seem to regard non-human creatures of all kinds as being very much second class citizens.

The official line among many of the candle burners and kneelers I have known in the past seems to be that animals, birds and fish were put on earth for us to do with as we will.

Personally, I think this is a dangerous and rather frightening attitude. How can anyone have anything but contempt for the malignant souled individuals who follow this appalling line of reasoning?

But then I have to admit that I do feel a pretty widespread contempt for most members of the established churches.

When did any church last make a united and public stand against vivisection, hunting or the many hideously cruel practises which are covered by the single word 'farming'?

(Come to think of it how often do churchmen and churchwomen take brave public stances on ethical and moral issues involving human beings?)

There is, it sometimes seems to me, a fairly widespread feeling among church people of numerous faiths that being a member of a church is an end in itself and something that offers instant moral superiority over all non church goers.

Too many of the churchgoing folk of the world seem to spend their days worrying about who has got the biggest spire and which congregation looks most prosperous when at worship.

I don't believe that these are issues which God finds important. Ask him yourself if you don't believe me.

The Underestimated Moral Argument

Pro-animal campaigners who oppose animal abuse in general and vivisection in particular have, in recent years, allowed themselves to be suckered into concentrating almost exclusively on scientific issues and arguments and virtually abandoning the moral issues. Moral and ethical arguments have been ignored; deemed to be less powerful than scientific arguments and therefore largely irrelevant.

This has been a huge mistake for the moral and ethical arguments are in many respects more powerful, more convincing and more difficult to oppose than the scientific arguments. It is impossible to nitpick or create false facts when arguing on moral or ethical grounds.

Our failure to utilise the moral and ethical arguments is, I believe, largely a result of the fact that the animal abusers and their allies and supporters know that they are more vulnerable when facing moral and ethical arguments.

It simply isn't possible to bend the truth so easily when discussing moral and ethical issues as it is when discussing scientific issues.

In concentrating on opposing vivisection solely with the scientific arguments we have fallen into a clever trap carefully laid by the pro-vivisectionists.

After a good deal of thought I have come to the conclusion that the scientific argument against vivisection tends to give vivisectionists an opportunity to marginalise their opponents and to trivialise the argument by concentrating on minor specifics.

Those of us who oppose animal experimentation will not ever win with the scientific argument alone because there will always be room for dispute and the vivisectionists will always be able to find doctors and scientists whose pro-vivisection views can be used to frighten and confuse the public.

As a result anti-vivisectionists end up spending much time arguing about obscure specifics. Often, there are no clear cut answers and as a result there must always be doubt in the uncommitted listener's mind – particularly since the vivisectionists are skilled at adding to the confusion with misleading, inaccurate and cruelly dishonest information.

Would a treatment for diabetes have been found earlier or later than it was if there had been no animal experiments in the 1920s? As an anti-vivisectionist I can produce evidence proving that the animal experiments delayed progress. But facts and evidence really aren't enough. The vivisectionists will do anything to win and since they are dishonest and (by definition) unethical and immoral people they will produce fake facts and create false theories to help them argue the opposite. The only half interested listener will be totally bewildered. He will eventually abdicate from taking any decision and allow himself to be bullied by the claims of the intellectual terrorists campaigning for vivisection who argue that to stop animal experiments would be to put at risk the health and survival of small children.

"If it's a choice between my child and a rat then I'll come down on the side of my child," the weary (and frightened) observer will insist.

It is possible that those who have chosen to argue exclusively on scientific grounds may have harmed the anti-vivisection cause and delayed the defeat of the barbarians.

Indeed, could it be that some of those who have promoted the scientific argument most ferociously (and who have insisted on totally excluding the moral arguments) might have been financed or in other ways supported by the vivisectionists? Some of those who have been most emphatic in their insistence that only the scientific argument is of value have also been the people most likely to attack others in the anti-vivisection movement. The infighting which has more or less destroyed the anti-vivisection movement in the last few decades appears to have come largely from those who have also insisted on following the scientific argument to the total exclusion of the moral argument.

Black And White

The ethical argument against vivisection is black and white (vivisection is immoral) and is constantly being strengthened by new evidence showing the extent to which animals have feelings and are (contrary to the claims of those who support vivisection, hunting and other obscenities) sentient creatures.

Ethical arguments are now regarded by some as being out of date and irrelevant but they are powerful and it is a mistake to neglect them. Even among the best scientists (and animal experiments are the refuge of the second and third rate scientists) scientific truths and methods are not real truths and have no permanence. They are regularly replaced as new discoveries are made. The only real truths are moral truths, the only unquestionable certainties relate to man's responsibilities, duties and rights.

It was, after all, the ethical argument which led to the defeat of the last great moral outrage – the slavery of black humans.

Anti-vivisectors have fought a losing battle for over a century because whether we like it not history is built upon perception not reality and myths can be more important than facts. True history is what we remember and what influences our lives. Facts are, of themselves, of considerably less significance than myths and perceived truths. A widely believed falsehood is more likely to prove influential than a little known truth.

If all else fails the vivisectors will happily lie (they are, by definition, intrinsically corrupt and intellectually barren but though they may be narrow-minded and prejudiced they are also sometimes cunning and exceedingly devious). For example, they will (and frequently do) argue that vivisection has helped us to conquer cancer when the facts show that the battle against cancer has been and is being lost. The myths and lies of the vivisectors have produced confusion but have also become gradually accepted as fact. There are many scientists, politicians, journalists and apparently well informed and reasonably intelligent individuals who seriously believe that laboratory experiments on animals are valid and essential.

(It is because perception is more important than reality that politicians use spin doctors. It is worth remembering that Goebbels is the spiritual father, and the patron devil, of all spin doctors.)

Chapter Three

The Scientific and Medical Arguments Used By Animal Abusers

The animal abusers try to support meat eating and vivisection with as many pseudo-scientific arguments as they can. They claim (quite falsely) that human beings need to eat meat, drink milk and eat eggs. They claim that vegetarians and vegans who do not eat meat, drink milk and eat eggs will suffer from vitamin, mineral and protein deficiencies. These are, to put it bluntly, lies for which there is no scientific basis.

Many of the lies told by animal abusers revolve around the use of animals in laboratory experiments.

The animal abusers ignore or defy the evidence and claim that vivisection is essential for the development of new forms of treatment. They argue that without vivisection we will never find a cure for cancer. (At the same time they usually manage to give the entirely false and unfounded idea that vivisection has already helped us find cures for many diseases, and is on the verge of helping us make great breakthroughs which will make cancer, heart disease and stress of nothing more than historical interest.)

Those with a personal, vested interest in the survival of the meat industry have started many rumours. It has, for example, been claimed (largely, I suspect, by people working for or paid by the meat industry) that people who do not eat meat must inevitably suffer from anaemia and other disorders.

(It is, incidentally, interesting to note that in my view the vast majority of the individuals who support and defend animal abuse do so because their wealth or jobs depend upon animal abuse. And an equally large proportion of the money used to defend animal abuse comes from corporations and individuals who have a vested interest in animal abuse. In contrast to this a massive majority of the individuals who oppose animal abuse do so in their own time and at their own personal expense – often taking personal risks to do so.)

The animal abusers much prefer scientific arguments to moral ones because it is much easier to create confusion when arguing on scientific grounds. Moral arguments – which are simply about what is right and what is wrong – leave relatively little room for discussion.

One big mistake many pro-animal campaigners make is to assume that science is based on truth – and that scientists are honest and honourable individuals for whom the truth is of paramount significance.

Sadly, this simply isn't true.

To begin with many scientists are only marginally competent. In my years of studying research reports published by vivisectors I have constantly been astonished by the lack of wisdom shown and have come to the conclusion that vivisection is a branch of science practised almost exclusively by second rate scientists of very moderate intelligence.

Vivisectors routinely make such crass and fundamental mistakes that even if their work were based on intelligent theories it would still be without value. For example, when performing their experiments they often make no allowance whatsoever for the fact that the animals they are using are extremely stressed and anxious because they have been removed from their friends and their normal environment. Nor do they seem to understand the significance of the relationship between diet and health. Bizarrely, it is by no means unusual for vivisectors to perform experiments without making sure that they take any note of the age or sex of the animals they are abusing. Vivisectors have such a false understanding of the animals they abuse that they deny that they have emotions (such as love and fear) and can feel pain. In addition, against all the available information, they falsely believe that there are anatomical and physiological similarities between animals and humans which are great enough for them to be able to draw conclusions about humans when experimenting on animals. If the vivisectors were not so cruel they would be pitiful.

Many scientists are fraudsters – little more than second rate crooks – and the scientific literature is littered with untruths and half truths.

The truth is that animal experiments have held back science for centuries. Two thousand years ago Galen dissected pigs. His work misled other doctors for a thousand years. The first attempts at blood transfusion ended in disaster because blood from animals was used. Vivisectors have, time and time again, misled doctors, delayed the development of useful treatments and been responsible for the deaths of countless thousands of human patients.

An Endless Variety Of Indignities

Many people don't understand exactly what sort of experiments animals are used for.

This is no accident. Many of those who want animal experiments to continue argue that the experiments are painless and that the animals do not suffer. The truth is very different. I have filing cabinets filled with research papers from universities and institutions around the world and there seems to be no end to the variety of indignities that researchers can think up for the unfortunate animals in their power. Most of these experiments are performed on your behalf and/or with your money.

If you are uncertain about the nature of vivisection then try imagining that you are taking part in a sensitisation test for a new perfume. This is a common and simple experiment.

First, scientists would shave a patch of your skin – removing every small hair – so that the perfume would make the best possible contact with your skin. Then they would put a large quantity of concentrated perfume onto your skin and leave it there. A plaster would be put over the test area to make sure that the perfume remained in the closest possible contact with your skin. You would be tied down to make sure that you didn't move about and disturb the experiment. Every few hours or so the test site would be inspected. And more of the concentrated perfume would be added until your skin went red and started to itch.

You would want to scratch but you wouldn't be able to. A thick dressing would be put over the test area and your hands would be tied to stop you interfering with the experiment. The itching would get worse and worse. But the scientists doing the experiment wouldn't give you anything to stop the itching because if they did they would interfere with their results.

Even if you cried and begged for mercy they would ignore you. These scientists are trained to ignore such pleas. It is their job to cause suffering – and to record the consequences.

Gradually, the area of skin under test would become redder and redder. Eventually it would probably begin to blister. Fluids would ooze out of your skin and drip out from underneath your plaster. You would probably notice some blood oozing out as well. Before long your whole body would probably begin to react. You might start to wheeze and to have difficulty in breathing. Your skin would start to burn and to itch and your heart might well start to pound.

The aim of a sensitisation experiment is deliberately to induce an allergy response by giving so much of the test product that the body responds violently.

You would feel ill. You would probably feel nauseated and you might start to vomit.

The scientists would refuse to give you any treatment in case it interfered with the test. Instead they would simply write down your symptoms and make notes about the condition of your skin. When they had acquired enough information they would kill you.

That is one of the simplest, commonest and least intrusive experiments vivisectors perform. If you were chosen for a more intrusive experiment scientists might deliberately make you blind by sewing up or removing one or both of your eyes. Or they might drill a hole into your skull, drop chemicals directly into your brain and then make notes about your response.

Well Looked After?

Vivisectors claim that the animals they torture and kill are well looked after before and during experiments. This is, as you might expect from people of this type, another lie.

The truth is that animals are often kept in tiny cages for years – alone, terrified and able to hear the screams and cries of those creatures ahead of them on the death list.

I've unearthed the official figures for the amount of floor space animals are allowed in laboratories – and the length of time they could spend in those cages.

Dog
Possible life expectancy: 35 years
Size of cage: 8 square feet

Rat
Possible life expectancy: 4 years
Size of cage: 0.4 square feet

Cat
Possible life expectancy: 20 years
Size of cage: 3 square feet

Mouse
Possible life expectancy: 3 years
Size of cage: 0.4 square feet

Rabbit
Possible life expectancy: 15 years
Size of cage: 3 square feet

Guinea pig
Possible life expectancy: 7 years
Size of cage: 0.7 square feet

Monkey
Possible life expectancy: 30 years
Size of cage: 6 square feet

Hamster
Possible life expectancy: 2 years
Size of cage: 0.34 square feet

You might like to measure out the size of these cages on your living room carpet. And then imagine the horror of your family dog or cat living in a cage like that for years – without love or companionship, in constant fear and probably in severe pain too. You will note that the amount of space officially allocated to a cat is probably not a good deal more than the amount of space available in the sort of box people use when transporting their cat to the vet or to a cattery.

Too Horrible To Contemplate

Sadly, very few people (even among those who are keen on seeing animal experiments stopped) are keen to read anything detailing what goes on in laboratories.

Animal lovers find books and articles (and photographs) detailing what goes on in laboratories just too horrible to contemplate. And people who don't love animals just don't care anyway.

Over the years I have come to the sad conclusion that writing and publishing books detailing the powerful scientific arguments against vivisection will never change anything.

No one who has read my books *Why Animal Experiments Must Stop* or *Betrayal of Trust* (both published by the European Medical Journal) could be in any doubt about the total futility of animal experimentation. The evidence in *Betrayal of Trust* totally demolishes the argument that vivisection is of value to human beings. But those books have not stopped animal experimentation – partly because not enough people are willing to read them, and partly because the supporters of vivisection refuse to discuss the main arguments which *Betrayal of Trust* raises.

Simply For Money

I believe that the majority of the scientists around the world who perform animal experiments do so largely for money. It is what they do for a living.

The vivisectors are committed to defending what they do for two reasons. First, if they admit that vivisection is scientifically invalid and morally wrong then they must also admit that what they have spent their lives doing was scientifically invalid and morally wrong. Second, if vivisection stops they will have to find another way to earn a living. And although vivisectors are an untalented and not terribly bright bunch vivisection does pay very well.

And so the vivisectors stick together. When they do bother to defend what they do (which isn't often) they either nitpick (deliberately confusing and boring the listeners) or they dismiss pro-animal campaigners as emotional individuals who care too much about animals.

They claim that anyone who doesn't agree with them is cranky, ill informed and led by their emotions. They seem to regard the whole subject as their territory and they sneer at anyone whose thinking contradicts theirs.

When I wrote a short one page paper opposing vivisection for a major international medical journal the journal published over a dozen pages of indignant rebuttal from vivisection supporters who had been shown my paper in advance of publication. (Needless to say I was not shown their responses or invited to defend myself.)

Deliberately Boring And Confusing The Public

The anti-vivisection movement has been for decades embroiled in a long lasting row with the corrupt and close minded 'scientific' establishment (which supports vivisection for clear financial reasons rather than for scientific reasons). Passion and fact have been overtaken by nit picking and a seemingly endless game of table tennis style arguments which have bored and confused the public and left the fundamental issues sunk in a sea of trivia. This is, of course, a deliberate policy by the vivisectionists.

It is important to remember that the establishment opposes pro-animal policies and the media protects the establishment. This is much easier to do with a scientific argument than with a moral argument.

Your Animal In Their Hands

The world's vivisectors – the evil, barbaric intellectually bereft individuals who perform allegedly scientific experiments on animals – torture and kill countless millions of animals every year.

Every thirty seconds these Mengele think alike pseudo intellectual thugs get through around one thousand cats, dogs, puppies, guinea pigs, baboons, chimpanzees, rabbits, hamsters, mice, rats and kittens.

They obviously need a constant supply of animals to satisfy their depraved needs.

They often obtain monkeys and other animals from countries where these animals breed naturally. In some countries animals of this type are treated like vermin and can be hunted, captured and sold with no restrictions.

Mice needed for experiments are often specially bred.

But finding enough dogs and cats can be difficult.

In America where there isn't quite as much secrecy about these things it is now known that vivisectors regularly torture and kill former family pets.

Amazingly, around two million pets are stolen every year in the US. In one part of New York over 10,000 dogs were reported missing in a single nine month period. One bereaved 'owner' searched for his missing dog and found him inside a research laboratory.

Vivisectors prefer working with family dogs and cats because they are tame and trusting – and less likely to bite or scratch. I firmly believe that petnapping goes on in Britain too. Tragically, I believe if your dog or cat goes out at night there is a real risk that he or she could be captured and sold to a laboratory. If a family animal has ever mysteriously disappeared it could have ended up in a vivisector's laboratory. I believe that because family dogs, cats and other animals are stolen to feed the apparently never ending demands for more laboratory fodder animal lovers who have lost pets should have the right to enter laboratories at any time to search for missing animals.

You Don't Need To Torture A Cat To Help A Cat (Any More Than You Need To Torture A Human Being To Help A Human Being)

Those who breed animals for experiments sometimes claim that the animals they breed and sell are used in experiments – for example to develop vaccines – which will eventually help other animals. I have, for example, heard it argued that cats which are bred for vivisection are used in experiments to help prepare vaccines which will help other cats.

This argument is often put forward by otherwise intelligent and thoughtful individuals as a reason why animal breeding centres should be allowed to remain in business.

The truth is, of course, that even if vaccines for cats are necessary and useful there is no need to breed cats in cages in order to do the experimental work that will help put the vaccines on the market. There are many vaccines on the market for human beings but as far as I am aware there are, as yet, no special farms in existence where human beings are bred and kept in cages so that they can be used in vaccine development.

If vaccines for humans can be prepared without experimental humans it is reasonable to assume that vaccines for cats can be prepared without experimental cats. (In order to keep this argument simple I have deliberately ignored the question of whether or not vaccines are of any value. I have dealt with this issue in other books.)

The Hidden Danger Of Animal Experimentation

There is growing evidence to support the contention that many of today's new and most threatening viral epidemics have been generated by medical scientists working with animals.

For example, during the 1960s and 1970s, encouraged by animal studies which they believed suggested that the sort of viruses they were working with were responsible for the development of cancer, researchers were trying to find an anti-cancer vaccine.

They combined viruses which were known to cause cancer in animals in an attempt to create new viruses which they hoped would give them some clues about how viruses caused cancer.

At the same time other researchers working for the military were trying to develop viral weapons with which opponents could be killed (and countries destabilised) *en masse*. Cancer researchers and scientists working for the military on the development of death bugs were, it is claimed, developing HIV like viruses in laboratories.

I believe it may have been through incompetence (a common fault among the mass of second-rate scientists around the world who routinely perform experiments on animals) that newly created viruses were inadvertently spread by contaminated vaccines.

No Compromise

Attempts have on several occasions been made to bring together vivisectionists and their opponents in an attempt to find a peaceful solution to the whole question of animal experimentation.

In my view these attempts have been tricks on the part of the vivisectionists: tricks which enable them to take the position that they are being conciliatory and trying to find a solution to a problem which they recognise exists.

There can be no compromise with the vivisectors. Animal experiments are scientifically worthless, morally repugnant and ethically inexcusable and they must be stopped.

The only solution I will accept is for vivisectors to stop their evil and pointless work. I will never negotiate with them because there can be no compromise on this issue. To look for a compromise with vivisectors would be like negotiating with gas chamber operatives during the second world war in a search for a compromise over the Holocaust.

Chapter Four

Profits From Animal Abuse And The Cost Of Caring

The animal abusers and their supporters will inevitably claim that if we stop using animals – and start treating them with respect – the effect on our economy will be disastrous. This is, of course, exactly the same argument which was used to support slavery. Black people in the US were told that their slavery was an 'economic necessity'. In Australia the aborigines were deprived of their birthright for economic reasons. In South Africa apartheid was considered necessary if the country was going to get richer. In all these instances, of course, the black people were not the beneficiaries.

It is perfectly true that if we stop abusing animals then many companies will make less money – and lots of individuals will lose their jobs.

In contrast, animals don't vote. They don't pay taxes. They cannot buy support. They don't employ lobbyists to work on their behalf. And they have too few supporters who are prepared to make their welfare a priority.

Poverty of the spirit, the true end result of animal abuse, is not a problem which concerns politicians.

For hunters, farmers and others to claim that their own particular form of animal abuse should be allowed to continue so that they can keep their jobs is an audacious example of self interest. It is exactly as though Nazi gas chamber operatives had claimed that they should be allowed to keep killing Jews so that they could keep their jobs.

But, although the financial argument is regarded as a powerful one by politicians, the fact is that it is not true that the human race must inevitably suffer enormous hardships if we stop using animals in the brutal and primitive way that we do now.

Since human needs and wants (for food, clothing, medicines and so on)

97

will not disappear the lacunae created by the disappearance of existing food, clothing and medical firms will quickly be replaced by other industries. Jobs lost will be replaced as new companies are born and grow.

It may be true that for a while we will all be slightly poorer and have a slightly lower standard of living if we stop abusing animals. But do we really want to be rich if being rich means that our wealth is built upon the immoral abuse of other species?

Financial Cost

Changing the status quo is always difficult, partly because change often makes people feel uncomfortable but also because change often means that people are exposed to a real personal, financial cost.

And I find it impossible to think of any change to the status quo that would cost as much in raw financial terms, or prove as painful to the economy, as changing the way that animals are treated.

The simple fact is that much of our society's wealth has always been built upon the exploitation of the weak.

For centuries many fortunes have been built upon the exploitation of weaker and less well educated nations. In America the immigrant whites took cruel advantage of the native Americans and the black slaves who were brought in to perform heavy manual labour. In Africa the immigrant whites took cruel advantage of the native Africans. In Australia the immigrant whites took cruel advantage of the native Australians. And, of course, the European nations succeeded in colonising much of the world; extracting and stealing the natural resources and exploiting and killing the local inhabitants.

We like to think that this is all part of history and that we have stopped exploiting weaker peoples but we haven't, of course.

The big drug companies exploit poorer nations by selling them drugs which are out of date or too dangerous to be accepted in so called civilised countries. Food companies exploit poorer nations by selling them prepackaged food (such as dried milk for babies) which is neither necessary nor good for them. Tobacco companies exploit poorer nations by encouraging their citizens to start smoking. At the same time as they are paying out huge amounts of compensation to smokers in 'developed' countries the tobacco companies are advertising and promoting tobacco consumption in undeveloped countries – often by encouraging the citizens of those countries to associate cigarette smoking with the comfort and wealth which is usually associated with the west.

Our scientists enabled us to turn relatively harmless local products (such as the opium poppy and the coca leaf) into potentially lethal products (morphine, heroin and cocaine) for our own western consumption. When it became clear that the consumption of these drugs could become a threat to economic growth (by destabilising work forces) we declared war on the countries where those raw products were grown and began to bomb and burn their farms so that we could destroy their natural crops.

A Widespread Dramatic Downturn Expected If Exploitation Is Halted

Quite a number of industries would suffer a dramatic downturn if animal abuse and exploitation were halted.

Zoos and circuses would have to close, of course, as would furriers and fur shops. The meat trade (including farmers, abattoirs, butchers shops, sausage and pie makers, animal feed suppliers and so on) would come to an abrupt end. Vets would take quite a financial hammering. The drug industry would lose out yet again because of a dramatic fall in the sales of antibiotics and other drugs given to animals. The food industry would have to change dramatically in order to survive. The leather goods industry (including shoe manufacturers) would also have to change in order to stay in business.

The meat industry is a vast consumer of transport vehicles. There would be no demand for lorries in which to transport animals if there was no animal trade.

There would be a temporary but massive rise in unemployment (although most of this unemployment would disappear as new industries arose and grew to satisfy the still existing needs of the community for food, clothing and entertainment). And, of course, governments everywhere would face a dramatic cut in tax revenues.

But a real man – and a real woman – is prepared to do the right thing whatever the cost.

Isn't it about time that we were led by real men and real women – instead of insignificant cardboard cut-outs?

Part Three

How And Why Animal Abusers Are Winning The Battle

Chapter One

Control Of The Media

The government does not want pro-animal campaigners to win and to threaten the status quo. It will do everything it can to make sure that pro-animal campaigns fail. By controlling the media, using force (through the police), using techniques such as marginalisation and, when necessary, simply removing the right to free speech, the government is determined to keep the upper hand.

Traditional forms of protest (such as marching in the streets with banners) are now no longer effective, unless the turn out is so huge that the government begins to worry about lost votes. Power is no longer about physical property, or even about wealth. It is more about how much media attention can be controlled.

It seems to me to be very clear that a government which is prepared to spend millions of pounds making sure that there is a huge police presence at every animal rights event (to make it clear to the world at large that pro-animal protestors are a dangerous bunch, to intimidate those who can be intimidated and to physically prevent some people reaching or speaking at protest sites) will spend public money suppressing the public's legal right to protest and will put a great deal of effort into controlling the media.

No Time For Values Or Policies

Political 'spin' is not a new concept. Josef Goebbels, Hitler's propaganda chief, was an early mass-media manipulator and image manager who would have found easy employment with any modern political party. Goebbels understood that the spin doctor's job is not just to create a positive image for his client but also to avoid unfavourable publicity. Damage limitation through news management is vital – particularly when image is all there is. The Labour

Party was the first political party in Britain to be built like a Hollywood film set – all front and no substance. Tony Blair and his Labour Party colleagues were the first political leaders in Britain to really understand how power can be obtained and retained through media manipulation. It was, I believe, because of this understanding that the Labour government, at the end of the twentieth century and the beginning of the twenty-first century, has worshipped so dutifully at the Church of St Rupert of Murdoch; the new twentieth century Sun King.

The Labour Party has very successfully controlled the media in Britain – partly through a series of headline catching promises, partly through judicious leaking of image boosting information, partly through using the old Nazi trick of distracting attention from one story by providing another story (Goebbels successfully drew attention away from the Holocaust by beginning a media campaign drawing attention to British atrocities in India and Palestine) and partly through doing financial deals with the media barons. ("Print good stuff about us and we'll make sure you don't have to worry about the Monopolies and Mergers Commission".)

The Labour Party has recognised that journalists need crises to dramatise the news (and to sell newspapers or attract viewers) while politicians need to seem to be responding to crises. Neither politicians nor journalists really care about whether or not the crises are solved. They are interested solely in the short term. Problems are not worth reporting until they become crises which can be dramatised. And politicians only react when a crisis has already developed. (Politicians often use crises to further extend their own power. When terrorists set off a bomb politicians often respond to the crisis by introducing rapidly drafted new laws which give them more power.)

Naturally, a government which only acts in a crisis never has time to study values or to make any meaningful public policies. Modern politicians, as exemplified by the Labour Party, always react and respond rather than lead.

Money Talks

It is true that money talks – but it doesn't always tell the truth.

Modern politicians often do deals with media magnates who are far more likely to have links with animal abusers than with pro-animal campaigners. The proprietor of the Daily Whatsit may not actually have a potted meat factory in the basement but he is quite likely to have financial links with companies which are dependent upon animal abuse. There is no real money to be made out of campaigning for animals and so there is no chance of a proprietor being manipulated or persuaded by any such link.

Politicians want publicity which draws attention towards their promises, and their apparent good intentions, and away from their failures and their broken promises. Journalists and their editors want eye catching headlines. The relationship between politicians and the media bosses is a symbiotic one: everyone involved benefits.

A Nation Of Couch Potatoes

Most modern homes have more media related equipment today than a major news room would have had less than a decade ago. It is not uncommon to find a suburban home with a satellite dish, computer, modem, fax machine, and mobile telephone.

But those who control the media still control the world because most people are entirely passive – they are 'couch potatoes'; they do not take an active part in the media revolution. Most people simply stare at the television unquestioningly. They rarely even listen to what is said. (Media specialists who advise people on how to use television will warn that it is only possible to get across one thought in a single programme. They therefore encourage their clients to repeat the same notion for as long as they are on the air – and to ignore the questions of the interviewer.)

Most people simply sit back and allow themselves to be fed information and views that their corporate and political masters wish them to be fed.

Sadly, it is difficult to underestimate the intelligence of the average human being. A recent survey in the US showed that nearly half of all Americans think that human beings were created by god within the last 10,000 years. (They probably also think that god was American, a burger-eating, country & western fan and lived in Texas.) Whether you favour the theory of evolution or the idea of creation this shows a remarkable lack of knowledge of history and is, I suspect, symptomatic of an equally remarkable lack of curiosity. (Even more extraordinary is the fact that a quarter of American college graduates – who, one might have assumed to be a little better educated – believe that humans were created by god within the last 10,000 years.)

Children have, it is true, learned to interact with the media technology but, on the whole, they restrict their interacting to playing computer games or surfing the net in search of pornography.

The Court Of Power

We have to fight our battle in what Marshall McLuhan described as "the real court of power, the media". That is, of course, the court of power which the establishment uses. They know that perception is everything and that the myth is often the reality.

Most people trustingly believe everything they read in their daily newspaper or see on television. This demonstrates an innocence which no doubt delights the authorities. The truth is that everything which appears in newspapers or on television has been carefully edited to satisfy the prejudices of the owners and their political allies.

I truly believe that the best and most honest, sources of information these days are small independent publishers and privately published newsletters which do not have any exclusive or close links with outside commercial companies. Such publications may contain bias and prejudices but at least the bias and the prejudices belong to the authors and publishers rather than to some outside source. The ordinary reader is today most likely to obtain access to the genuine, underlying realities behind the 'news' through privately published newsletters and small presses.

Television: The Low Point

Television is probably the worst offender in the media.

Have you ever wondered how news crews so often happen to be in the right place at the right time when something newsworthy happens?

There are two explanations for this apparently inexplicable anomaly.

First, television stations are frequently given advance notice of events which politicians or others regard as newsworthy. News shows on television frequently broadcast pre-packaged interviews which they have been given by companies or political parties. Interviewers are told to toe the line and to be polite if they want to get any exclusive interviews in the future.

Second, if an impromptu event is missed the news crew can always recreate it. It is not unknown for TV producers to recreate news items they have missed or been unable to film.

Superficially Convincing

Goebbels believed that Nazi media campaigns did not have to stand up to close examination as long as they were superficially convincing. This is, of course, exactly the same philosophy which is espoused both by the supporters of vivisection (who use the technique of intellectual terrorism to persuade people that animal experiments are essential and potentially life saving) and politicians (who simply make new promises when it becomes apparent that the public no longer believes their old promises, rightly assuming that most people are trusting and do not believe that even politicians could possibly dare to lie all the time).

Goebbels believed that primitive arguments were the most effective.

Ignorance And Misinformation

Most people say nothing about cruelty to animals for three reasons.

First, they often don't know what goes on in laboratories, in abattoirs and on farms and in other centres of animal abuse.

Second, they don't believe that animals are capable of suffering.

Third, they do believe that using animals – even if unpleasant – is essential. They falsely believe that without eating meat they will die. They falsely believe that if experiments are not performed on animals then their children will die slow and painful deaths.

The key factor here is, of course, ignorance. But the ignorance is compounded by misinformation.

Keep On Taking The Tabloids

Broadsheet newspapers, TV stations and radio stations have obeyed commercial dictates and followed a strictly pro-animal abuse agenda for many years.

Even the language used in broadsheet newspapers seems designed to affect the way in which readers respond to what they read. While writing this book, for example, I read about mink kept four to a cage in a farm where mink were bred to be turned into fur coats. The journalist who wrote the article described the caged mink as 'snuggling' up to one another in their tiny cages. The word 'snuggling' suggests cosy and comfortable informality. The reality is that the mink probably didn't have much choice about whether they 'snuggled' up to one another or not.

It is rare indeed for any broadsheet newspaper to publish any pro-animal sentiments.

Over the years tabloid newspapers have always been far more willing to publish pro-animal campaign stories. This is for two reasons. First, the so called redtop tabloid newspapers, having much larger circulations, are less dependent on advertising revenue and can take a tougher line with big, powerful corporations. Second, the popular newspapers (which have a large readership) are more likely to publish stories which their editors feel might appeal to their readers rather than their advertisers.

This revelation may come as something of a surprise to many of those pro-animal campaigners who routinely buy and read broadsheet newspapers in the mistaken belief that they are more likely to provide an honest and fair interpretation of the news than tabloid newspapers.

Broadsheet newspapers – having smaller budgets and more space to fill, as well as a smaller inclination to upset powerful commercial advertisers – are far more likely to publish pre-packaged press releases and one sided articles glorifying animal research, genetic engineering or some other wonder of science than are the tabloids.

Broadsheets, although often vapid, bland and unimaginative, are even more likely to bend, spin and manipulate the news for their own purposes than are the tabloids.

Tabloids are often regarded as being unbelievable compared to the mainstream media, but if the same story appears in a tabloid and a broadsheet newspaper, and there are factual differences between the two stories, then it is safe to assume that the story in the tabloid is the accurate one.

I am not suggesting that tabloids always tell the truth. But they certainly tell the truth more often than the broadsheets (or 'unpopulars' as they are sometimes known). There is, indeed, a strong argument to be made that real journalism (including investigative journalism) now only exists in the tabloid newspapers.

I first learned the truth about the broadsheets a couple of decades or so ago when I was invited to write an article about 24 hours in the life of a hospital casualty department for a weekly magazine published by a broadsheet newspaper. The 24 hours I spent in the hospital casualty department was relatively quiet and the article I wrote described the air of expectation, the boredom, and the waiting rather than the excitement, the violence, the fear, the blood and the death that the editors had obviously expected.

Disappointed by the lack of action the magazine editor told me to go back, spend more time in the casualty department and wait for something exciting to happen. He wanted me to 'create' an exciting but 'fake' 24 hour period. In my innocence I was horrified and refused to do as he asked. Naturally, the article never appeared in print. Reality is often just not exciting enough.

What many readers forget is that the sole function of the modern media is to make money; it will do this more easily by amusing and diverting readers and viewers than by providing them with genuine information.

Broadsheets pretend to be eager to provide their readers with the truth but in reality they often stagger from day to day alternately scaring and then reassuring their readers. Scientific research is regularly and widely misused in order to help corporations and politicians to fulfil their objectives. Many people still believe that the words 'scientific research' guarantee the quality and provenance of the information which accompanies it. Sadly this simply isn't true. Large companies know that they can obtain whatever scientific results they want merely by hiring the right scientists. Scientific fraud is commonplace even in academic circles and so it is hardly surprising that when a company tells its highly paid scientists to find evidence proving that its new product is safe the scientists will find a way to do what they are told. Nearly all published and promoted scientific research these days is patently self-serving.

Media Manipulation

Surveys and polls are another easy way to manipulate the media. Ask the right questions and you can get exactly the results you want. Concocted and inaccurate surveys taint our perceptions of the truth and distort public debates. Once a survey has found its way into the public consciousness it is exceedingly difficult (or even impossible) to remove it.

And so vivisectionists will conduct surveys proving that scientists, doctors and members of the public all think that animal experiments are essential. They do this by asking the right questions.

For example, if you ask the question: "Do you agree that experiments on rats should be continued so that doctors can find new treatments to help save the lives of children with leukaemia?" the majority of the people being questioned will respond as the questioner wants them to respond.

The broadsheet papers are written largely by pro-establishment conservatives and they are written for people with many well-established, traditional prejudices. These people have, of course, already been taken in by the 'let's keep abusing animals' arguments. (They often have a personal financial interest in maintaining and spreading these arguments. For example, many medical and science journalists do additional – and frequently well paid work – for drug companies or for magazines and newspapers which obtain financial support from the drug industry.)

The broadsheets trivialise arguments just as much as the tabloids but they tend to do it less skilfully, with less flair and with less fairness. The tabloids may appear to be hysterical but they are more likely to be independent and they are, therefore, more likely to publish material which is sympathetic to the pro-animal cause.

The broadsheet newspapers are, I believe, more likely to be edited by pro-hunting animal abusers and because they do not pay as well as the tabloids, they may be staffed by second-rate journalists and columnists who are far less intelligent than their tabloid counterparts (and more likely to be taken in by false arguments).

News Into Drama

Boring political news was first turned into dramatic and exciting and readable material by Joseph Pulitzer in the US. In 1883 he bought the *New York World* and started turning straight news stories into drama. He gave dull stories plots and turned dull characters into actors in the dramas. He introduced conflict and ensured that his stories were packed with colourful details. He made his stories even more dramatic by giving them loud, clever, irresistible headlines, illustrating them with photographs and adding graphics too. He (and his newspaper) turned institutional minutiae into emotional, sensational and immediate news.

In recent decades the growth of television (and, in particular, of 24 hour news television) has increased the need for drama in the news. And since camera crews can't be everywhere at once it has meant that the news has become steadily more and more stage managed. Lobbyists, special interest groups and big business PR departments have all learned the way to play the game – and have all learned how to put forward their own versions of reality.

Image makers for big corporations use a vast armoury of tricks to deflect criticism, and to improve the public perception of their products and their companies. Most big corporations will go along with whichever politicians are in power. Opposing governments has never been a good way to get (or stay) rich.

The press is used to promote public illusions and to help maintain private privilege. Appearance and reality are now further apart than at any time in history. The media today has, by its willingness to take part in this gross deceit, corrupted democracy, enabled politicians to lie and survive, and cheated the public. Newspapers, radio and television disseminate the news they are given but they do not disseminate the truth. The propaganda is spread faithfully but the substance is ignored. Real, underlying conflict is glossed over.

Subtleties Are Important

The way in which the news is presented can have a tremendous impact on the way it is received. Apparently small, subtle changes can make a huge difference to the way readers and viewers form their opinions.

For example, people who read a headline which says "Animal experiments are worthless" are less likely to believe that animal experiments are worthless than are people who read a headline which says "Are animal experiments worthless?"

And, curiously, research has shown that a denial in a headline doesn't make much difference to the way in which those who read it will perceive it. So, for example, most people who read the headline "Vivisectors deny that animal experiments are useless" will, nevertheless, believe that animal experiments are useless.

People tend to believe what they read in a headline wherever they read it. Even if they see it in a newspaper for which they have little or no respect the chances are high that they will still believe it. People who read the underlying story are unlikely to be convinced by the facts if they have already read a headline. And people who only read the headline will, of course, go away with the headline's message firmly implanted in their minds.

Many people say that they do not read newspapers at all. Or that they ignore certain classes of newspaper. Unless they never go into newsagents shops those people are deluding themselves. Research done in the US has shown that people who read (or glance at) headlines, but don't read the stories accompanying those headlines, will believe the messages in the headlines. Mass, subliminal messages can easily be spread through newspaper headlines.

It Is Essential To Make People Think

In order to produce change it is necessary to create phrases which make people think.

People tend to listen to, take note of, and to remember rhetoric and promises rather than facts. To ignore these sad facts is to say 'no' to the possibility of power.

One of the most effective ways to have an impact is to take two words which don't normally go together (for example the words 'smart' and 'drugs') and then use them to make a phrase. The phrase 'smart drugs' is eye and mind catching because the combination of these two words is thought provoking.

My own favourite phrase is 'intellectual terrorism'. I coined this phrase some years ago and use it to describe the actions of the animal abusers when they try to frighten people into accepting that vivisection is essential by telling them that if animal experiments are stopped their children may die of terrible diseases.

By accusing those who use this argument of 'intellectual terrorism' we quickly and easily put them on the defensive. Even more important is the fact that such phrases, once used, tend to stick in the listener's brain. Once there they are difficult to remove.

The phrase 'animal abuser', which I have used throughout this book to describe anyone who opposes animal rights, also has a powerful impact and should, I believe, be used widely by those who want to further the rights of animals. Anyone who opposes animal rights can safely and accurately be described as an animal abuser.

Some time ago I was surprised when I received a furious telephone call from an editor who had on his desk something I had written. The item which had made him so upset was a short piece in which I made the point that butchers shops which display skinless corpses are offensive to large parts of the community. The editor's complaint was about the entirely accurate phrase 'skinless corpse' which he said he found deeply offensive.

The lesson here is simple: we should use the phrase 'skinless corpse' as often as possible since it reminds meat eaters that what they are eating was once a living, sentient being.

(The long established comments "I don't eat anything with eyes" and "I don't eat my friends" are provocative and useful. I also like to tell people that "I don't eat humans or animals".)

We Have To Shock

We have to be more prepared to shock if we are to combat the media manipulators who are controlling our lives (and enabling the animal abusers to stay in business).

For example, it is widely believed by the British people that Princess Diana was murdered. Polls show that around 98% of the British population believe that she was killed by the British Secret Service. Tony Blair was Prime Minister when Diana died and the Labour Party was in power. That's all we have to say. We can safely let people draw their own conclusions.

Many pro-animal campaigners try to be tactful when complaining about the way other nations treat animals. The time for tact has gone. Diplomacy has got us nowhere. The Spanish people claim to be the most religious in Europe. And yet they treat animals in a way that makes it clear that they are still barbarians. They honour their matadors as heroes. We should not be shy about describing matadors (and others involved in the bullfight business) as little more than cowardly and overpaid abattoir workers. The Spanish depend very much on the income they gain from British tourists. Let us try to persuade holidaymakers to boycott Spain. A similar, tough approach can be used against other nations where cruelty to animals is endemic.

Use New Techniques To Spread Messages

If you bring together two images which are not usually thought of as being associated with one another then the brain of the person who is fed the resultant composite image will be shocked. The owner of the brain will find it difficult to get rid of the image. This can be useful because shocking and surprising images often make the reader think carefully. Research has shown that images which do not fit the norm require the creation of special new neural pathways just to be evaluated. And so shocking and startling images often last for a long time – as well as making the reader more vulnerable and open to other new ideas.

It was for this reason that in my book *Fighting for Animals* (published by the European Medical Journal) I used beautiful pictures of animals in serene surroundings to illustrate hideous quotes from vivisection research papers.

When talking or writing about important issues it can also help to try putting a vision within a vision. ("I was in my car, driving from London to Birmingham, when I found myself thinking back to a time when, in 1987 I...") This is another extremely effective way to imprint messages on the listeners brain when telling them something you want them to remember. (But beware – this technique is extremely effective. US President Reagan is reported to have once tried using this technique but ended up putting himself into a trance and losing his train of thought completely.)

News Management

We have to be prepared to manage the news more effectively.

The myth about AIDS and heterosexuals was devised because gay activists realised that they would get nowhere if AIDS remained a gay disease. I remember doing a radio broadcast with a gay activist after I had written a number of articles arguing that AIDS seems far more likely to be transmitted via sexual activities such as anal intercourse which result in bleeding and which are popular with homosexuals, than it is to be transmitted by other forms of sexual intercourse. After the broadcast the campaigner agreed with me that I was absolutely right and told me that he and other gays had agreed that in order to get funding for AIDS research they had to turn AIDS into a disease which was perceived as being a threat to heterosexuals as well as a threat to homosexuals.

The 'AIDS kills heterosexuals' campaign was so convincing and so effective (despite the absence of supporting scientific evidence) that most journalists and politicians ended up believing it. For several years I was widely vilified in the press and on TV for having dared to tell the truth about the disease. (Many TV producers allegedly making open-minded programmes about AIDS refused to let me onto their programmes unless I promised not to discuss the possibility that AIDS might not be a major threat to heterosexuals. The result was, of course, that the myth was strengthened still further.) I can understand why gay activists did what they did. And it was an extremely effective manipulation.

Pro-animal campaigners also have to learn how to manage the news.

Vivisectionists will frequently argue that animal experiments save patients lives. They will refer to individual cases of patients alleged to have been saved by animal experimentation. This is, of course, absolute nonsense. No animal experiment has ever been responsible for saving or even helping to save a patient's life. We have to counter these absurd (but often believed) claims by referring to individual patients who have been killed or injured by misleading animal experimentation. This isn't difficult to do. (Readers will find case histories of patients who were killed by animal experimentation in my book *How To Stop Your Doctor Killing You*, published by the European Medical Journal.)

Meat trade promoters sell their product by warning consumers that without meat and meat products they will become vitamin or mineral deficient. We have to counter this absurd lie with the truth: that eating meat is unhealthy and that those who follow a vegan or vegetarian diet are much less likely to become deficient in essential vitamins and minerals.

Perception Or Truth

As any student of history will confirm the reality is that the truth is far less important than the reader's perception of the truth. Naturally, the media manipulators take full advantage of this. They know that headline readers tend to believe a headline whatever the underlying facts may be.

So, when politicians and cosmetic companies in the UK agreed to a modest reduction in the number of animals used in experiments headlines appeared which suggested that animal experiments were being stopped altogether. In reality the change meant that the millions of animals being tortured and killed would be reduced by between 250 and 300 a year but that wasn't the impression given when the story appeared in the newspapers.

The story as it was run benefited three groups of people. The cosmetics companies looked good. The politicians managed to grab the glory and look good (and they succeeded in distracting attention away from the fact that they had failed to create a Royal Commission to investigate the scientific value of vivisection – as they had promised to do before they were elected to power). And editors had a grabby headline which helped them sell newspapers. Very few readers who saw the headlines realised that hardly anything had changed.

This was a perfect example of perception winning over truth. Everyone involved knew that the headlines were self aggrandising manipulations – created simply for the way they would benefit businesses and politicians and distract attention from the real issues and the real truths – but no one cared about that.

Politicians have created a culture of deceit, trickery and lying and the media has been a willing helper.

It is a grave mistake to assume that truth alone is enough to enable us to win on behalf of the animals. Sadly, many aspects of the truth are irrelevant. You may or may not agree with it, but in political terms the important thing in this world is perception – not truth. (Though, of course, if the truth is widely publicised it can have an important effect on perception.)

The fact is that reality has not helped us win freedom and respect for animals. For centuries now pro-animal campaigners have been relying solely on the truth – and getting nowhere. One problem is that the truth is often unpleasant and unpalatable. Many people do not want – and cannot cope with – the truth.

For example, pro-animal campaigners have often published horrific photographs of animals in distress. Many books and leaflets have been published showing pictures of animals in cages or laboratories. But sensitive and caring individuals find such photographs too awful to look at. And, by definition, insensitive and uncaring individuals simply do not care.

Pro-animal campaigners have published books and numerous articles proving that meat causes cancer, and that animal experiments are not just worthless but are actually a hazard to human health. But time and time again the truth has been defeated by perception. The lies told by the animal abusers have consistently defeated the truths told by the pro-animal campaigners.

Historians know well that history is all about myths and perceptions and has very little to do with the real truth. We have to be aware that although the truth is important, and will eventually bring light to the darkest corner, perception is often more important than truth when we are trying to change the present and improve the future.

We Have To Work Together

The real tragedy is that those human beings who protest on behalf of animals would have probably won battle victories some years ago (and maybe even a victory in the major war against animal cruelty) if they had worked together.

But pro-animal campaigners fight one another even more fiercely than they fight the animal abusers.

During the years in which I have been fighting for animals I have lost count of the number of lies which have been told about me by people who describe themselves as caring about animals. There are some individuals, allegedly members of the animal rights movement, who are apparently driven by little other than vanity, and who spend most of their time (and the money they can raise from others) vilifying those who put their heart and soul into fighting for animals.

The individuals who snipe and whinge and back stab always attack any new attempt to defeat animal abuse (though they are themselves always slow to come forward when leaflets have to be handed out, envelopes stuffed or print bills paid). They always seem quick to identify difficulties and they always concentrate on the problems not the possibilities.

But what have the sceptics got to offer which is better?

Maybe they are content with the thought that the animal abusers are a dying breed. Maybe they comfort themselves with the thought that since the animal abusers usually eat meat they will die younger of cancer, heart disease and other serious disorders. Maybe they are content to trust in the hope that vegetarians and vegans will live longer, be stronger and will eventually take over the world.

I find it impossible to take such a relaxed attitude about the cruelty which exists in our world.

Every day vivisectors around the world torture and kill one thousand animals every thirty seconds. Countless millions of animals live short miserable lives in terrible conditions so that they can be slaughtered and turned into hamburgers. Our streets are decorated with skinless corpses, hanging inside and outside butchers shops and apparently causing little or no revulsion among the nearby shoppers. Ruthless farmers, who would do anything for money, cram wild animals into tiny cages so that rich women can wander through the streets (past the butchers shops where the skinless corpses are displayed) in fur coats.

It was reported that when two women were running an animal rights stall in London a policeman ordered them to remove a poster showing a cow on a slaughter line. Shackled and suspended upside down by a back leg, her throat had just been stabbed by the slaughterman and blood was oozing from the wound: the daily reality in hundreds of UK killing plants. The officer said the image was 'offensive' to the public and it had to come down.

"But just along the road", one of the women said to the policeman, "there's a butcher's shop with decapitated pigs hanging on a hook in the window. All their feet have been broken and half hacked off. I find that offensive and upsetting."

The policeman did not change his mind. His mind was closed on the subject.

It is, surely, that sort of inbuilt, long-standing, prejudice; that blindness; which we should be fighting.

How much longer are we going to allow the in-fighting to continue?

The Press Complaints Commission

In an article, in which I attacked hunting and animal experimentation, I warned readers that meat causes cancer. I wrote, quite accurately, that there is: "evidence available to show that people who eat meat are far more likely to get cancer and die young".

I wasn't particularly surprised when the Meat and Livestock Commission complained to Britain's Press Complaints Commission (PCC) saying: "The claims made in the article are both damaging to the industry and could be greatly disturbing to the public...".

The PCC asked for evidence supporting my statement that: "young people who eat meat are far more likely to get cancer and die young."

I sent several pages of scientific references, including a seven year study of 35,460 people, published in the journal *Cancer Research*. The scientists who wrote that report concluded: "it is quite clear that these results are supportive of the hypothesis that beef, meat and saturated fat or fat in general are etiologically related to colon cancer."

There isn't room here to list all the scientific references I sent in support of my claim. But the Press Complaints Commission found in favour of the Meat and Livestock Commission. They reported that the MLC: "denied that there was any evidence to link the consumption of meat with the cause of cancer".

I asked the PCC what medical or scientific proof the MLC had provided to support their claim that meat does not cause cancer.

I asked if any members of the PCC had medical qualifications.

And I asked if the PCC had hired any medical or scientific experts to look at the references I sent supporting my statement that meat does cause cancer.

I also sent the PCC photocopies of more journal articles proving that meat causes cancer.

The copies included one published in the *British Medical Journal* which stated: "previous studies...have shown a reduction in all cause, cancer and cardiovascular mortality among people who do not eat meat".

I also sent papers from the *Journal of the National Cancer Institute* ("animal fat, especially from red meat, is associated with an elevated risk of advanced prostate cancer"); the *New England Journal of Medicine* ("animal fat was positively associated with the risk of colon cancer") and the *International Journal of Cancer* ("frequent consumption of...red meat is a risk factor for colo-rectal cancer").

In its judgement the PCC complained that my article contained: "no acknowledgement of any opposing view".

I found that rather surprising. My original comments had been made in a newspaper column. I was hired, and paid, to present my personal opinions to my readers. It was perfectly clear that the column was not intended to offer a balanced viewpoint.

Drama critics, book reviewers, sports reporters and political commentators are not expected to acknowledge opposing views in their articles. Cookery writers who publish meat recipes are not instructed to include vegetarian recipes for vegetarians. But, according to the Press Complaints Commission, if I write an article about meat I am not allowed to state my view that meat is dangerous without reminding readers that the Meat and Livestock Commission does not agree with me. I am supposed to remember · that the meat industry might suffer financial loss if I attack it. (The PCC seemed to ignore the fact that if I make statements which are false I can be sued for libel.)

It is my view that by upholding the meat industry protest the Press Complaints Commission may (if it has any influence at all) have helped to delay the dissemination of the truth and to dissuade other writers from repeating the well established fact that meat causes cancer. How many unnecessary deaths do the PCC members now have on their conscience?

(It is, incidentally, interesting to note that in a full page advertisement in the *Financial Times* in November 1998 it was reported that advertising bought for the Meat & Livestock Commission had won an award as one of 1998's most effective advertising campaigns. The FT advertisement included this citation: "Advertising from 1994-97 supported the meat market from a barrage of social, ethical and economic factors and the biggest ever health scare to hit any food market – BSE. Advertising reduced the impact of these factors, slowed the rate of decline in red meat eating and in 1997 restored the market to year-on-year growth. A total media spend in the period of £36.2 million resulted in additional red meat sales of £739 million, a return of nearly 18 to 1.")

Does the PCC really need to protect the meat industry from me?

(The editor of the newspaper concerned refused to publish a column in which I attacked the PCC. I resigned.)

Misled, Lied To And Manipulated

The public is constantly being misled, lied to and manipulated. Most branches of the news media are unfair, inaccurate, contentious and under the control of powerful institutions which adhere faithfully to well hidden agendas.

Generally speaking, the editors of broadsheet newspapers and the producers of radio programmes and television programmes can be considered to be pro-establishment, pro-status quo and pro-animal abuse. If a pro-animal campaigner is quoted on animal issues (such as vivisection) his remarks will invariably either be accompanied by some patronising or disparaging note or by disapproving comments by an alleged expert who holds an opposing (pro-animal abuse) viewpoint. On the other hand when a pro-animal abuse individual is quoted the remarks will invariably be quoted without comment, criticism or qualification.

The animal abusers have so successfully established the belief that animals are here to be used that most allegedly independent commentators find it difficult to accept that there can possibly be any alternative to animal abuse. When, on a rare radio interview I opposed the intellectual terrorism of vivisection and calmly and quietly explained why vivisection is not, never has been and never can be of any value to human beings, the allegedly independent presenter, who was perhaps aggrieved because he had been unable to destroy my arguments, ended the interview by describing me as 'controversial' and reminding the listeners that I had been 'expressing a personal view'.

Quality Of Reporting Set To Decline Still Further

I wish our news media could be forced to identify the source and sponsor of every piece of news they print. A news story which had the source of the press release printed at the bottom of it would be far more honest than the present system.

That won't happen. It would not be in the interests of the media and it would not be in the interests of the sources of the stories.

Nor will our media ever become more responsible or deliberate than they are at the moment. Speed is the very essence of the newsroom and the demand for more new information is constant and insatiable. As the number of television channels, radio stations and publications increases so the demand for more information (and for 'exclusives' or 'scoops') will also increase. Ethics and moral values will take even more of a back seat. The quality of reporting is set to decline a good deal further in the coming years.

Animal Abusers Control The Media

The animal abusers and their supporters (and I include politicians among those supporters) have successfully taken overall control of the media. If those of us who campaign on behalf of animals are to win the war against animal abuse then we have to do something non-violent but dramatic. We have to prove to the politicians, and the business leaders who approve of animal abuse, that pro-animal campaigners can no longer be ignored.

In our present climate the directions of change are managed by those who are most skilful at feeding the media with the news it needs – and who are most skilful in manipulating whatever crises develop to their own advantage. Propagandists and lobbyists ultimately rule our world because they control both the media and the politicians.

Pro-animal campaigners constantly lose these battles because of a failure to understand how to control all aspects of the modern game. The animal abusers are more skilful at managing crises and manipulating the media and they generally win these exchanges.

Intellectual And Emotional Terrorism

One of the classic false arguments used by animal abusers is to warn anyone thinking of joining or supporting the animal rights movement in general, and the anti-vivisection campaign in particular, that if they oppose animal experiments (and are successful in calling for an end to animal experiments) they will, inevitably, be exposing themselves and their families to the risk that when they fall ill they will be deprived of life saving treatments which would have been available had scientists been allowed to continue performing animal experiments.

"Of course we all love animals," the hypocritical animal abusers will claim. "We all wish that animal experiments weren't necessary. But the sad fact is that animal experiments are essential if we are to find a cure for (and here the animal abuser will insert a popular or fashionable disease or the name of the disease of which he knows the listener is frightened or the name of the disease which he knows already affects the listener or a member of his family) then animal experiments simply must continue."

This technique, which I describe as 'intellectual terrorism', works well for the animal abusers. It frightens ordinary people who may not have access to the facts and it undoubtedly frightens many who are simply so afraid of disease and death that they will cling to any hope which is offered.

A commonly used extension of this technique is to tell anti-vivisection campaigners that if they are going to be true to their beliefs, and not take advantage of the experiments on animals which have been done, then they (and their families) have to refuse to accept any modern medical treatment.

This despicable and utterly ruthless trick, which I consider to be cruel and brutal as well as thoroughly dishonest, frightens many and puts many more off the idea of opposing animal experimentation.

Not long ago vivisectionists issued 'Animal Research Abolition Cards'. The cards contained the following message: "To honour my belief that animal research should be abolished, I hereby pledge that: In the event of accident or emergency, I will refuse all medical treatments developed or tested on animals, including but not limited to: blood transfusion, anaesthetics, anticoagulants, antibiotics, sutures, open heart and other types of surgery. If my child suffers from a genetic illness or other serious condition, I will not allow them to have life saving treatment developed through animal research. None of my pets shall receive any veterinary vaccine or medicine that has been developed or tested on animals."

These cards were sent to those who oppose animal experimentation with the suggestion that they sign them.

As I believe vivisectionists ought to know perfectly well, the evidence shows quite clearly that animal experiments are without value to doctors or patients. (Two vivisectionists once appeared on a TV programme with me where the whole issue was debated – at the end of the programme, when viewers were asked to vote on the issue, I, who had argued that animal experiments are of no value, have never been of value and never will be of value, received 84% of the vote.)

But the creator of this card had avoided this slight technical problem by including the phrase 'developed or tested on animals', thereby neatly side stepping the issue of whether animal experiments had been of any value whatsoever.

I am appalled by this specialised type of what I consider to be intellectual terrorism.

Many caring and active anti-vivisectionists have died prematurely because they have been encouraged, quite falsely, to believe that all modern medical treatments have been developed as a result of animal experimentation. Many people who care about animals do refuse essential treatment, do suffer unnecessarily (and probably do die prematurely) because they have believed this piece of nonsensical and mischievous animal abuse propaganda. For example, a well known comedian and author reported that his wife had died from cancer, having refused to use any known medicines that had been used in animal experimentation. "It wasn't easy for her," wrote the comedian, "but she died with a clear conscience."

I have, over the years, received numerous letters from readers suffering from serious health problems telling me that they are refusing to take drugs which have been tested on animals. I usually try to write back to such correspondents and point out that my view is that since animal experiments are entirely pointless there is absolutely no need for any animal lover to refuse to take a drug which may have a beneficial effect on his or her health.

I also point out that if someone who cares about animals dies prematurely (for no good reason) then animals will be losing another champion.

I believe that those who are guilty of originating and perpetuating this type of intellectual terrorism are directly responsible for many deaths.

Deceit And Trickery

This cruel variety of pro-vivisection propaganda is based on a hypothesis that has been proved to be entirely false. All the available evidence shows (quite conclusively and, I believe, beyond argument or dispute) that animal experiments are not, never have been and never will be, of any value whatsoever to doctors or patients. I have for years successfully argued that no vivisector has ever produced any evidence which is of value. (No vivisectionist has ever beaten me in debate on this issue and these days they are so tired of defeat – and embarrassed at having no evidence to support their outrageous contentions – that they refuse to debate with me.)

Indeed, on the contrary, the evidence shows that the drug industry's reliance on animal experimentation when developing and testing new drugs is one of the main reasons why at least one in six patients in hospital are there because they have been made ill by doctors; why forty per cent of people who are given prescription drugs suffer notable and sometimes lethal side effects and why, if a patient who is receiving orthodox medical treatment develops new symptoms, the chances are that the new symptoms are caused by the treatment for the original symptoms.

Emotional Blackmail

Animal abusers use other types of intellectual terrorism.

For example, a favourite trick which is often used by hunt supporters and zoo owners, is to warn that if they are forced to go out of business they will kill all the animals in their care.

"If you stop us hunting," the hunters will say, "we will have to kill all our horses and dogs."

"If you make us close down our zoo," the zoo keepers will argue, "we will have to kill the lions, the tigers, the monkeys, the elephants and all the other animals."

The animal abusers usually expose their own sense of brutality by adding an extra vicious twist to their cruelty and claiming that all this means that the pro-animal campaigners will be directly responsible for the deaths of any animals which are killed.

"We don't want to kill our animals," the hunters and zoo keepers will claim. "We love our animals," they will say. "And if you force us to kill them their blood will be on your hands."

This is, of course, all a total nonsense.

If and when hunts and zoos are closed down it will not be necessary to kill any animals.

Finally, I frequently receive letters from animal abusers who claim that if we all stopped eating animal then sheep, pigs and cows would become extinct. 'If animals weren't put here to be eaten, why were they put here?' argue the animal abusers.

The answer to this is simple. We don't eat rats, mice or foxes and they aren't extinct.

Chapter Two

Control Of The Police And The Courts, Manipulation Of Justice And The End Of Freedom Of Speech

Much unhappiness and frustration is caused by the fact that in our society the law is commonly confused with justice, liberty, freedom and equality.

In truth the law has very little to do with these fundamental moral principles. The law exists to help society defend itself; it is used by those who represent society as a weapon with which to dominate and discriminate against individual powers and freedoms. The law is man's inadequate attempt to turn justice – an abstract theoretical concept – into practical reality. Sadly, it is invariably inspired more by the prejudices and self interest of the law makers than by respect or concern for the rights of innocent individuals.

These misconceptions about the purpose of our law lead to much disappointment. And these misconceptions help to create a considerable amount of underlying stress.

No society has ever had as many laws as we have and yet few societies can have ever had less justice.

Many of the laws which exist today were created not to protect individuals or communities but to protect the system. It is because such crimes threaten the security and sanctity of the system that theft and fraud often attract harsher sentences than crimes such as rape and murder which affect individuals. Crimes against the individual are seen as less important than crimes against society because the rights of the individual are seen (by society) as being of less significance than the rights of society.

The irony is that although the law was originally introduced to protect individuals the law has itself become a tyrant. Today, few individuals can afford to take advantage of the protection offered by the law. The law oppresses the weak, the poor and the powerless and sustains itself and the powers which preserve it. The enormous costs of litigation mean that there is one law for the rich and no law at all for the poor. The result is that the law threatens and reduces the rights of the weak and strengthens and augments the rights of the powerful.

Things are made worse by the fact that the people employed by society to uphold and administer the law on behalf of ordinary people too often take advantage of their positions to abuse their powers. The interpretation of the law is so often at the discretion of those who are paid to uphold it that those who have been hired by society become the law itself.

Too often society allows officers of the courts to abuse their power to satisfy their own personal ambitions, grievances and prejudices. In return society, in its broadest and most undemocratic and domineering sense, is protected by the people who benefit from its patronage. It is the worst sort of symbiotic relationship.

The final irony is that as respect for the law (and those hired to uphold it) diminishes so the divide between the law and justice grows ever wider.

When people who are given the power to protect society disapprove of something which threatens their status they introduce a new law. As political parties come and go so we accumulate layer after layer of new laws. It doesn't matter if the new laws conflict with the old laws as long as all the laws help to strengthen the status of the state.

Meanwhile, as the oppression of individuals continues, lawlessness (and disrespect for the law) grows among officials and those in power. Brutality, arrogance, corruption and hypocrisy have all damaged public faith in the law but the only response from society has been to create new laws to outlaw disapproval. Society's primary interest is to protect itself and society is not concerned with justice, freedom or equality since those are values which are appreciated only by individuals. Those who have power are concerned only with their own survival and with perpetuating their power. The simple truth is that we live in a corrupt society which takes little or no account of the needs or the rights of ordinary people.

In a strange way all this should provide us with some comfort. When the oppressive forces of a society try to suppress information and free speech it invariably means that they are worried. Ridicule is usually the first weapon used by cruel oppressors. Violence, imprisonment and the suppression of free speech usually only come when the establishment is fighting a rearguard action.

The Greatest Threat To Liberty

We like to think that the Germans who worked in the concentration camps were exceptionally evil individuals. But every nation contains thousands of pustulant thugs who will obey orders as long as they're paid well, given heaps of authority and provided with smart uniforms.

If the British government decided to exterminate beggars or Jews they would find it easy to recruit staff. Most of those who satisfy the requirements for gas chamber attendants are currently working as lawyers, policemen and traffic wardens. And in their hands this island is rapidly becoming a police state.

For years politicians and lawyers (two words which, I feel, go together like 'vomit' and 'floorcloth') have been doing their efficient best to take away all your rights.

Today, the greatest threat to your liberty comes not from criminals but from the legal system. New laws now mean that you're guilty if the police say you're guilty. Human rights have been replaced by police rights. I know of parents who do not like their children going out at night – not because they are frightened of thugs and muggers because they are frightened that their children will be beaten up by the police. Many policemen seem to feel that they have to be confrontational. Instead of simply being there, holding back, or even backing away from trouble, the police seem inclined to provoke trouble and to exacerbate difficult situations. I suspect that this may, to a large extent, be a consequence of bad management and bad training. The *Police Service Statement of Common Purpose and Values* states that the police must: "...strive to reduce the fears of the public and, so far as we can, to reflect their priorities in the action we take" and that policemen and policewomen should be: "...compassionate, courteous and patient, acting without fear or favour or prejudice to the rights of others."

Those paid to run the legal system have forgotten that the law was invented to protect the ordinary citizen. (They also seem to have forgotten that they are giving more and more power to a bunch of people who are often largely little more than corrupt, racist thugs.) Even a former Conservative Home Office Minister has warned that: "giving the police extensive power could be bad for decent folk as well as criminals."

Too Many Laws And Not Enough Justice

Recent governments have passed endless oppressive and unjust laws and in consequence the prison population is rising so fast that it won't be long before prisoners will have to come outside and law abiding citizens will have to go inside.

Ring up and complain that you've been robbed, mugged or raped and a snotty, supercilious, patronising, overpaid individual with an 'I'm-far-too-busy-and-important-to-be-dealing-with-your-piddling-little-problem' voice will reluctantly take down your details before explaining that they're far too busy to do anything about your complaint.

But leave your car outside the police station while you go inside to complain that you've been assaulted and when you get back to it you'll find that someone has found the time to give you a ticket.

Motorists are easy targets. Most ordinary citizens have an in-built fear of authority and a long established respect for the law. It's far easier to make the crime statistics look good by catching a few generally law abiding middle class motorists than it is to try and catch potentially troublesome criminals.

Vandalism is now so commonplace that churches are installing video cameras. They are, presumably, worried that they'll turn up one morning and find the church gone and the spire propped up on bricks.

A Reputation For Brutality And Cruelty

The police are rapidly and widely acquiring a fearsome reputation for brutality and cruelty. It seems to me that a large proportion of the men (and women) in the police force today would be criminals if they weren't in the police force. Joining up and wearing a police uniform is, today, an excuse for legalised thuggery. Most ordinary people today would feel more secure if we had fewer police and more justice

According to the *Police Service Statement of Common Purpose and Values* the aim of the police is: "...to protect, help and reassure the community: and to be seen to do all this with integrity, common sense and sound judgement."

The Public Order Act

Police commonly use sections 2,3,4 and 5 of the Public Order Act 1986 when dealing with demonstrators.

Section 2 (1) of the Act states: "Where 3 or more persons who are present together use or threaten unlawful violence and the conduct of them (taken together) is such as would cause a person of reasonable firmness present at the scene to fear for his personal safety, each of the persons using or threatening unlawful violence is guilty of violent disorder."

Section 2 (2) of the same act states that: "It is immaterial whether or not the 3 or more use or threaten unlawful violence simultaneously.

Section 2 (3) states that: "No person of reasonable firmness need actually be, or be likely to be, present at the scene.

Section 2 (4) states that: "violent disorder may be committed in private as well as in public places'.

And Section 2 (5) states: "A person guilty of violent disorder is liable on conviction on indictment to imprisonment for a term not exceeding 5 years or a fine or both..."

Does this mean that if three people are sitting together in their living room and Tony Blair appears, smiling smarmily and uninvited, on their TV set and one of the people watching the television announces to the others that he would like to force the grotesque Blair person to eat all his broken promises all three could be sent to prison for five years?

I have to confess that like much modern legislation the Public Order Act 1986 reminds me more of something penned by Lewis Carroll in one of his more imaginative moments than of any sort of legal document.

Harassment And Distress

I have met and talked to photographers in different parts of the United Kingdom whose homes have been raided by the police looking for photographs which could be used to help them arrest demonstrators. (The police did not have warrants). Press photographers have had their film seized – and have been jailed. In addition I have been told that it is not unknown for the police to demand film taken by press cameramen at animal rights demonstrations.

A video cameraman reported in the autumn of 1998 that he has been arrested six times in two years while trying to do his job as a video journalist. "Problems began," he reported, "two years ago when I was arrested at a hunt, for causing "alarm, harassment and distress – I had pointed my camera at a huntsman."

"After talking to colleagues," he continued, "it transpires that I am not alone. Journalists from all sections of the print and broadcast media who report on direct-action protests involving the police are systematically being bullied, harassed, assaulted and arrested."

The police are, it seems, using the new Protection from Harassment Act (which was originally intended to protect women from stalkers) to control photographers and cameramen who try to report the way that the police deal with demonstrators.

A photographer who took pictures of the eviction of protestors from

Manchester Airport in 1997 reported that he was arrested for obstruction and had his equipment and film confiscated – even though he claimed that he had cooperated fully with the demands of bailiffs and had shown his press card. He was put in prison for 14 hours and later convicted in court of obstruction of bailiffs, with a conditional discharge.

There are stories of police officers arresting camera operators, removing tape and then denying that there was ever tape in the camera in the first place. At least one video cameraman now has a colleague filming him while he films the action so that he has some evidence about exactly what has happened. One cameraman has evidence that the police actively erased taped footage which they didn't want to be shown. Another cameraman was arrested for filming protestors destroying crops from a genetics test site. He was locked up for 24 hours and police then obtained authorisation to hold him for another 12 hours (something usually only granted in cases of terrorism). All his clothes were taken from him and he was forced to wear a paper suit.

A freelance reporter was charged with breach of the peace while covering a secret conference of senior politicians and businessmen. He was held for several hours after he had knocked on neighbouring doors to see if residents had seen anything.

Citizens Fight Back

More and more citizens are suing the police for wrongful arrest, for assault and for other breaches of the law. In 1998 it was reported that the Manchester police had paid out £10,593,573.90 in damages and costs in one case alone. In 1996-7 Scotland Yard paid out more than £2.4 million in damages to settle claims, including assault and false imprisonment. In December 1998 *The Times* reported that: "The government faces a bill of up to £50 million in costs and compensation for miscarriages of justice uncovered by corruption investigators. The estimate was based on the possibility that 200 cases being investigated would all result in quashed convictions. The Times reported that: "Many of the allegations involve the fabrication of evidence, such as planting weapons, and in at least one case tampering with scientific evidence."

Planting weapons and tampering with scientific evidence can hardly be described as anything but dishonest and yet it is extremely rare for police officers to be sent to prison – even when convictions which have been obtained falsely have been reversed. Members of the public might wonder why.

Another question which needs to be asked is: "Why are damages awarded against the police, because of police incompetence or dishonesty, paid out of public money?" The average police officer would surely be far more careful

– and far less likely to fabricate evidence – if he knew that he was going to have to pay any damages awarded against him. It is difficult to see why police officers should not be held personally responsible for their own actions. If a doctor or accountant is found guilty of some wrongdoing then he will be held responsible for whatever financial costs may result. When a doctor is sued for making a mistake, or for some dishonest action, the taxpayer does not have to pay the bill. Why should the taxpayer have to pay when a police officer is found guilty of making a serious mistake – or, worse still, of corruption?

The present system ensures that the public suffer constantly. Members of the public pay the wages of the police officer who beats up members of the public and then members of the public pay the legal costs and damages awarded against the errant police officer.

Incidentally, policemen and traffic wardens are quick to grovel if they think they're dealing with someone whom they regard as important. A few years ago I acquired a large and impressive looking Buckingham Palace car park pass for the windscreen of my car. I quickly discovered that once they saw the sticker traffic wardens treated me very reverentially. For example, when on a book promotion tour I could find nowhere to leave my car I parked inside a shopping arcade. When I returned to the vehicle I found a traffic warden waiting for me. But he didn't give me a ticket. Instead he stopped the traffic while I reversed out of the arcade. He then saluted while I drove away, leaving him enveloped in blue exhaust smoke.

When I lost my sticker I had a flag made. In the place where the queen's car flies a royal standard I fly a skull and crossbones. I regularly get saluted by officials in uniform.

It is now a mistake to confuse the law with justice, liberty, freedom and equality. Today's law has very little to do with these fundamental moral principles. As H. L .Mencken wrote: "All governments, of course, are against liberty."

The Self Interest Of The Law-Makers

The law, man's inadequate attempt to turn justice into practical reality, is inspired more by the self interest of the lawmakers than by respect or concern for human rights.

This is why protest with a purpose attracts far more attention than mindless vandalism. And animal rights protests certainly do seem to attract more than their fair share of police attention.

If animal rights activists do £50 worth of damage to a building where evil people are doing indefensible and unspeakable things to animals the whole area will turn blue with policemen looking for clues. On the other hand, on several occasions when vandals did hundreds of pounds worth of damage to my office we were not visited by police officers until a few days after the incidents.

When a pro-animal campaigner did several thousand pounds worth of damage to vehicles belonging to a butcher he was arrested, taken to court and sent to prison for longer than the average murderer or rapist would expect to get. When £10,000 worth of damage was done to my car the police would not even bother to come and inspect the damage – let alone look for a culprit.

When a pro-animal campaigner threw a stone while attending a demonstration at a site where animals were being abused she was arrested and told to expect a five year jail sentence. (No one had been injured by the stone). When a fisherman repeatedly threw stones at me (I had been standing near the river in which he was fishing and was, he claimed, alerting the fish by my presence) I telephoned the local constabulary to report the incident. The police refused to attend on the grounds that I had not been injured by any of the thrown stones.

When vivisectors receive threats (however mild) these are invariably treated extremely seriously by the police. When I received and reported a written death threat (the writer claimed that he and his friends had hired a hit man to kill me because of my opposition to hunting) the police dealt with the matter (quite slowly) through the mail. I was never offered any form of protection.

And, of course, there are always thousands of highly paid policemen and policewomen available to protect lorries transporting animals, or to protect establishments where animals are being tortured and killed or reared for torturing and killing. In the north of England a small demonstration of less than 50 animal rights protestors was met with a police 'army' estimated to consist of 200 officers, including 20 on horseback.

The use of vast numbers of police officers to control protests organised by animal rights campaigners is even more remarkable considering the fact that, as far as I am aware, no one has yet been killed or injured by an animal rights protestor. (I think it is fair to say that this shows great reserve, good sense, compassion and patience on the side of the animal rights supporters.)

Those who oppose campaigns to close animal breeding centres, where animals are bred for vivisection, torture and death, argue that even if all the animal breeding farms in Britain were closed down the vivisectors would simply import animals from foreign breeding farms. This is akin to arguing that there is no point at all in Britain having rules about child labour or racism or the exploitation of the mentally retarded because even if we stop these outrages here they will still continue in other countries.

If we don't set a good example who will? If we don't start the tide of public opinion against animal abuse in Britain where will it start? If Germany has gas chambers for killing Jews does that mean that we have to have them too?

The Law Oppresses The Weak

Laws were originally introduced to protect individuals but 'the law' has itself become one of modern society's greatest tyrants. The law now oppresses the weak, the poor and the powerless, and sustains itself and the powers which preserve it. The law threatens and reduces the rights of the weak and strengthens and augments the rights of the powerful. At peaceful pro-animal rallies and demonstrations the police turn up armed with riot shields, full body armour, helmets, batons and CS gas. When one remembers that, as far as I am aware, animal rights campaigners have never killed (or seriously injured) any animal abusers (or police officers) this dramatic overkill seems to me to take on clear political overtones.

As political parties come and go so we accumulate layer after layer of new laws. We are now all living in one huge concentration camp. And as the oppression of individuals continues, lawlessness grows among officials and those in power.

Brutality, arrogance, corruption and hypocrisy have all damaged public faith in the law but the only response from the establishment has been to create new laws to outlaw disapproval.

The primary interest of the legal establishment is, it seems to me, to protect itself. The legal establishment does not appear to be concerned with justice, freedom or equality since those are values which give strength to you and me.

The Injustice Of The Law

The law has very little to do with fundamental moral principles. We may like to think that the law exists to protect us from the evil, the dangerous, the dishonest and the wicked but, sadly, this simply isn't true any more. Laws are created not to protect ordinary citizens, or their rights, but to protect international corporations, and their rights. Politicians and law enforcement agencies no longer seem to be concerned with protecting the electorate. Today, they're committed to defending 'society' and its corporate sponsors. It is in the interests of the politicians to create new laws because when there are many laws in a society (and so many laws that not even the lawyers know what they all are) then everyone will be bound to be a criminal. When every citizen is a criminal, or a potential criminal, the judiciary and the police, and therefore the politicians, have more power.

As respect for the law (and those hired to uphold it) diminishes so the divide between the law and justice grows ever wider.

Meanwhile, as the oppression of individuals continues, lawlessness (and disrespect for the law) grows among officials and those in power. Brutality, arrogance, corruption and hypocrisy have all damaged public faith in the law but the only response from society has been to create new laws to outlaw disapproval.

Society's primary interest is to protect itself. Those who have power are concerned only with their own survival and with perpetuating their power. The simple truth is that we live in a corrupt society.

The Police: The Enemy Of The People

The police probably do not think of themselves as behaving in an evil and reprehensibly immoral manner. Most of them never question what they have been told – or what they are told to do. People who join the police forces are probably not the sort of people who usually question authority.

The police who batter and beat up pro-animal campaigners at rallies and demonstrations may have been told that the people they are battering and beating up are all dangerous lunatics who love animals more than people. They have probably been told that without laboratory experiments on cats and dogs their children will all die of terrible diseases.

Many police officers tend to be insensitive folk of modest intellect. (Would a sensitive, intelligent individual want to join the police force these days?). Most probably do not have enquiring minds. They are likely to believe what they are told. They probably do not have the intelligence to realise that the people they are attacking are not only their real employers but are the 'good guys'.

Police Brutality Is A Major Problem

Pro-animal campaigners are not dangerous in the sense the police think they are dangerous. In a purely physical sense pro-animal campaigners are probably far less of a threat than football crowds or hordes of shoppers queuing for a big store sale to open.

I have received many reports of the police attacking and brutalising innocent demonstrators – many of whom are middle aged or elderly. I have little personal doubt that the police break the law far more often than the citizens they are supposed to be policing.

At one demonstration a girl was arrested for not removing her face mask. She was carried upside down to police vans. The police claimed that the girl was offending the public by wearing the mask, though there were only police and protestors in the area.

A policeman was seen to kick a demonstrator in the back and then stand there, camera in hand, waiting for a response. The same police officer was also alleged to have punched a young woman. I have heard of a policeman at a demonstration attempting to arrest a young woman for wearing a scarf. All this may sound unbelievable. But I believe it is true.

Is it not behaviour likely to cause a breach of the peace when several hundred police officers, some on horseback, many dressed in riot gear, surround a peaceful gathering? If a group of military-style demonstrators dressed this way surrounded another group of perfectly innocent citizens, who were exercising their right to meet and listen to speakers, would it not be realistic to describe the military-style demonstrators as guilty of 'behaviour likely to cause a breach of the peace'?

Are Pro-Animal Campaigners Targeted By The Police?

Why are so many police used at pro-animal demonstrations? Can it really be that there are not enough murders, rapes, muggings, burglaries and so on to keep them busy?

Of course not.

Politicians have argued that a large police presence is needed at demonstrations because of violence at pro-animal gatherings. It is true that there are always a few arrests at pro-animal demonstrations but it would be surprising if this were not the case when such confrontational tactics are used.

The fact is that (as I have said earlier) I am not aware of any one ever being killed as a direct result of any action initiated by pro-animal campaigners.

Indeed, there is evidence to show that alleged violent actions against animal abusers have been organised either by provocateurs or by animal abusers themselves. (One hunt supporter was jailed for nine months for placing a home made bomb under his own vehicle and then claiming that the bomb was the work of pro-animal activists.)

I have little doubt that the police, undoubtedly under instructions from their political masters, are targeting pro-animal campaigners in a particularly ruthless and inexcusable way.

Readers of mine have reported that they have been searched when travelling to pro-animal demonstrations. And I have also received reports that the police have raided the homes of pro-animal campaigners after they have attended demonstrations. (The police use the photographs they take of people and vehicles to enable them to identify protestors). I have even heard of pro-animal campaigners who have been taken to court simply for reporting animal rights activity.

When police identified a 12 year old girl and a 10 year old boy whom they claimed had allegedly thrown objects during a demonstration they picked up both children.

Detectives travelled some distance to arrest the girl. They called at the family home and intended to pick the girl up at her school until the girl's mother complained. The mother was allowed to pick her daughter up from school herself and to take her to a local police station on condition that the girl's grandmother went with the police to the station. The girl's mother was not allowed in the interview room with her daughter and the girl's grandmother. When a solicitor was requested they were told they would have to wait hours for one. "She was hungry and tired and really wanted to go home so she let them interview her," said the girl's mother.

The 10 year old boy was stopped by police officers as he and his mother were about to board a coach. The boy was grabbed, read his rights and told he was under arrest. He was told that he was under arrest because there was video evidence of him throwing a stone at an animal rights demonstration. He and his mother were put into a police van and held in a cell for seven hours before the boy was interviewed, fingerprinted, photographed and formally cautioned. "I don't know whether he threw a stone," his mother is reported to have said. "He admitted it during the interview but any child would have admitted to anything to get out of there."

It seems surprising to me that the police should have taken so much trouble over children alleged to have thrown stones (but not as far as I am aware, to have injured anyone or caused any damage). Is it now official police policy to arrest every child in the country who is believed to have thrown a stone? Or are the police only interested in arresting children who throw stones while attending animal rights demonstrations? If there is a difference, why is there a difference?

One animal rights campaigner believes that the police are: "trying to frighten off old age pensioners and people with children so that they can pigeonhole everyone on demonstrations as young unemployed dreadlocked hippies."

My own feeling is that there is probably a good deal of truth in this allegation. Some law abiding citizens are now wary of attending animal rights protests because they fear for their own safety (they are, I need hardly add, frightened of the police, not of other demonstrators) and they fear that they may be falsely arrested and in consequence lose their jobs. This is, of course, all part of the marginalisation process. One community pillar told me that he didn't dare attend a demonstration because of his responsible post. In fact, of course, his responsible post gave him extra power and made him an even more potent demonstrator than he might otherwise have been.

Heavy-Handed Policing

Of the many readers who have written to me to complain of the heavy handed attitude of the police quite a number have claimed that in their view the police have deliberately started trouble at demonstrations – sometimes using provocateurs dressed up as protestors and sometimes merely behaving in a provocative manner.

Here is what one reader told me:

"I was stood by a gate watching the throngs of animal rights protestors milling about, waving banners and chanting when without any warning I was suddenly blinded and my face was burning. Also my hand had been hit with what I imagine was a baton. After the idiotic police started behaving like this the crowd became incensed. We are innocent and a threat to nobody. I and my partner suffered the effects of the CS gas well into the night and even the next day. I have seen statements from members of the police force which are fabrications, lies and massive exaggerations."

This reader told me that the CS gas was sprayed less than three feet away from where he was standing, that no warning was given, there was no danger to anyone's life and that no after care was offered.

At pro-animal demonstrations I have attended there have invariably been a large number of police cameramen in attendance – some equipped with video cameras and some with still cameras.

(I understand that there is still some question about whether or not the police are entitled to video and photograph innocent citizens – and to then make copies of the video tapes they record and the photographs they take. According to Liberty of the National Council for Civil Liberties, the organisation which protects civil liberties and promotes human rights, the police have to destroy fingerprints taken of people who have been arrested but subsequently not charged with a criminal offence but there is no provision for the destruction of video tapes.)

In my experience the police are too often arrogant and most unlike public servants. Two senior officers both refused to give me their badge numbers when I asked for this information. From the evidence I have seen I have absolutely no doubt whatsoever that the police cause most (if not all) of the trouble at animal rights demonstrations. And I have absolutely no doubt that police officers regularly lie when giving evidence to the courts.

Who pays for all this? Who pays for the massive police turn out, the helicopters, the vehicles, the horses and the cameras? I find it difficult to believe that local police forces can afford this massive expenditure out of their own budgets. I suspect that the money comes from some special Home Office budget.

If several hundred police officers surrounded a Parent Teacher's Association meeting there would undoubtedly be some conflict. If five hundred police in riot gear walked onto a railway station platform or a seaside beach there would be trouble. If a thousand police officers surrounded a meeting of a Women's Institute group, or turned up at a village cricket match, there would be some arrests. The current policy is self perpetuating. The police turn up and push demonstrators around. The police are, quite unnecessarily in my view, issued with full body armour and all police horses are fitted with visors. (This, despite the fact that I have no knowledge of any police officer or police horse ever being attacked). The police push and hassle and arrest any demonstrators who protest or try to protect themselves and thereby give themselves an excuse for a massive police presence at the next demonstration. The arrests enable the police to justify their actions and help them to further marginalise the pro-animal campaigners.

If they must attend demonstrations in such vast numbers, in order to satisfy their political masters and their commercial string pullers, the police, in their own best interests, really should learn to be a little more sensitive and to stay calm.

However, it is probably a lot easier for bully boy police officers to take on law abiding pro-animal campaigners than it would be for them to try to stop a crowd of young, fit, strong, belligerent football fans. Or, indeed, for them to try to arrest dangerous burglars who might be armed and ready to fight back.

Policing a pro-animal demonstration – attended by gentle, kindly, law abiding citizens – seems to give the police a good opportunity for truncheon and boot swinging exercises – with little risk to themselves. Several eyewitnesses have told me that in their view the police seemed to enjoy brutalising the weak and the defenceless.

Here is how one pro-animal campaigner described how the police treated her and other demonstrations at one protest:

"...after linking arms they proceeded to push everyone along the road. If you were too slow or got caught up behind other people, dogs etc you were shoved very roughly in your back to make you move forward, the further we walked the quicker they wanted us to move. When there are a large number of people and the police decide to close in from the back and sides you do not have much of an option on where to go. What I found to be totally unacceptable was the bullying behaviour, intimidation, bad language and total disregard for our well-being. I was brought up to respect our police force for the difficult job they do and the way they handle it – not any more. We were herded along like common criminals, pushed and shoved so roughly that some of us fell down on the road and you were not able to escape out of it (if you wanted to get out of the way or were pushed on to the side of the pavement where other police were, they simply shoved you back in the road)."

"It seemed as if the police use their own provocative actions to try and cause trouble and retaliation so that they can justify their huge numbers and expense. Why else, when the protestors entered the town square were there so many police; mounted police, police in riot gear and police dogs, was this to show the people how dangerous we are, so need to be controlled?"

And here is an extract from another letter I received from an animal lover who attended a pro-animal demonstration:

"I adore animals and have four rescue cats and have done numerous voluntary jobs working with rescue animals but I had never ever in my entire life attended any demonstrations before....I was totally horrified at the amount of police that was there, also the helicopter, video cameras, police on police horses...what this must have cost I dread to think. Most of all I was sickened to see the way the police treated the demonstrators and also the dreadful abuse that all of us were encountering from the onlookers."

"It started, my personal experience with the police, after the speeches. As you know we all marched through the town to go to the farm and we were all cut off at a certain point so we could get no where near it, obviously. On our return back from the cut off point to return to our minibus my daughter, fiance and I were at the tail end of the demonstrators to return when four policemen/women on horses suddenly were pushing all of us to one side with their batons and horses so as a car could come by, which it did. Then another car wanted to come by ten minutes after the previous one, so the same thing happened again, the police on the horses pushing us to one side. However the car was coming a little faster than the previous one. I just managed to push my daughter to one side and managed to get my body out of the way but did not get my foot away in time when the car went over my right foot. It was the front wheel, the passengers side. At the same time one of the policemen on the horses gripped hold of my left wrist, yanked my arm up and started to kick me endlessly with his foot and stirrup and then hitting me extremely hard endlessly with his baton even after the car had gone and my foot released. He finally let me go, laughing away to himself and his colleagues and some of the demonstrators got hold of me quickly and were hugging me and pulling me away quick in

case he returned. I was in so much pain with my arm and also with my foot. I was also in total shock as this was a serious assault that he did and for no reason whatsoever. By this time I was sobbing violently and I was also wondering why I was being led away so quick by the demonstrators. They told me when I asked that they were trying to lose me in the crowd because the policeman might return for more. I was absolutely shocked. When I returned to the bus the pain in my foot had gone but my arm was paining me too much, the pain was unbearable so I looked at it and showed the 14 others that were on my bus. It was dreadful, the whole of my upper arm was swollen and was getting bluer and blacker by the minute and I had to take pain killers."

"Dr Coleman this has not put me off at all. This is the beginning for me. I will be attending the next demonstration. Dr Coleman how can human beings do these things? I just can't stop thinking about all this. Most nights I lie awake just sobbing until I fall asleep. Please excuse my writing etc...I am still in a state."

Another reader wrote to me to say:

"A friend and I were on the pavement, to our left were a group of four people when out of the blue an unmarked police car came onto the pavement, two police officers got out, one of them was so out of order, he decided he was going to make an arrest no matter what and chose to pick on the young man in the group of four. The officer's manner was offensive, to say the least, and when I asked why he was acting this way I was told to mind my own business. As his manner became more offensive by the minute I asked him for his number and was told in no uncertain manner that he did not have to give his number to the "likes of me". What he meant by that is a puzzle as I am just a middle aged-housewife, with a deep love of all animals, who has spent the last ten years rescuing sick and abandoned cats from the streets of London."

Here is another extract from a letter from an animal lover:

"I can't understand why police always take such an aggressive attitude towards those who want to prevent animal abuse. Speaking as someone who has had cracked ribs, bruising etc because of the... heavy handedness towards those demonstrating against cruelty, I am very wary whenever a policeman comes near me."

I believe that by causing as much inconvenience as possible to local people the police are trying to further marginalise pro-animal campaigners. I suspect that this backfires quite often. Here is what one letter writer had to say:

"Returning back to my car after the march I noticed an elderly lady looking quite distressed behind her garden wall. I went up to her and apologised for so many people being in her lovely village on a Sunday afternoon and asked her if she knew why. She immediately said that... the only people she objected to were all the police milling about and not caring where they parked their vehicles."

This letter writer went on to say:

"I was threatened with arrest for standing observing how four policemen might treat one young man they had on the ground, shirt pulled down to his arms to immobilise him, knee in

the back etc. I was ordered to "join the rest of them'. I asked why I should move. The policeman threatened me with arrest... The attitude of the government, police etc make me all the more determined to continue with my fight against animal abuse."

Here is another letter from a pro-animal campaigner:

"I was suddenly jumped on by a policeman disguised as an activist. I struggled and swore and he got very heavy. I ended up in handcuffs and received some nasty bruises from the encounter. He told me that he enjoyed hurting me. I was kept in the cells for ages, like they always do. I was done for section 5 of the public order act and received a conditional discharge and £30 costs. A very small case – after all, I took no action – but that policeman was unnecessarily violent. I'd like to point out that I'm 51 years old and 5 foot tall."

A reader wrote to tell me about an experience she had when standing on a kerb opposite a farm where week old calves were being sent abroad for veal crates. She was, she wrote, hemmed in by the police standing in the gutter in front of her and by a high hedge behind her.

"I was standing near the edge of the pavement holding a cardboard placard when my foot slipped off the pavement. The police officer standing in front of me pulled me across the road to a police van. When he was asked what was happening he angrily shouted that I had assaulted him with the placard."

"I was taken to a police station, searched and put into a cell. After an hour or so I was questioned by the arresting officer. At around 11.00 pm I was handed back my handbag and told I would be released. After the police officer had checked with the inspector I was informed I was to be charged. They took my finger prints and photograph. I left the police station at about midnight for a one and a half hour drive home."

"There were always arrests... Often (sometimes if there were only twenty protestors there) there would be six police horses and two or three large white police vans. One police officer was heard to remark one evening: "We'll get them one by one'. There was a policeman there posing as a protestor."

"The man who runs the farm has been fined many times for animal cruelty."

"I was acquitted when the case came to court and all my witnesses had their expenses paid."

Two readers of mine visited a farm with a third friend, intending to demonstrate peacefully, and stood opposite the property for two minutes. They were then approached by a Chief Inspector and two constables and shown an official police document which stated: *"You are gathered at the venue of a private dwelling. You, by your presence in a crowd of demonstrators may be committing an offence under the Protection From Harrassment [sic] Act 1997. I require you to leave this area forthwith as your continued presence may intimidate the occupiers. If you fail now to leave, I will have no option but to exercise a power of arrest. You may then face criminal proceedings. I ask that you quietly leave the area now."*

One of these readers told me that she did not have an opportunity to walk away but was told that if she did so (i.e. she did what the police wanted her to do) she would be arrested. She was then asked for her name and address. When she queried the necessity for this she was told that she would be arrested if she did not comply. (I understand that members of the public do not have to give their names and addresses unless arrested or suspected of committing a crime.) She was, therefore, threatened with arrest on two separate occasions within a short space of time – despite the fact that she does not seem to have broken any law. And she was forced to give her name and address though it is difficult to see why this was necessary. The other reader pointed out that there were only three of them present and that this could hardly be described as a 'crowd'. She also wondered (in her letter to me) why the police were waiting at a farm where no demonstration was planned.

A pro-animal campaigner who suffers from kidney failure and who has to use a dialysis machine four times a day, was arrested when approaching a pro-animal demonstration because he had his dialysis equipment with him. A policeman is alleged to have demanded to know what the dialysis boxes in the back of his car were for and to have then arrested the pro-animal demonstrator for 'going equipped'.

This campaigner has so far been convicted eight times of obstructing a public highway. On one occasion he was arrested and convicted for handing out leaflets.

(Handing out leaflets can be an expensive business these days. In some areas of the country campaigners who want to hand out leaflets complaining about cruelty to animals now have to pay a fee of up to £100 for the privilege of enjoying their freedom to campaign.)

It would certainly appear to me, from the mail I have received, that enormous amounts of public money are being spent on using the police to protect animal abusers – and to harass pro-animal campaigners.

Surprise And Indignation

I have quoted so many of these letters (a small fraction of the total number of similar letters I have received on this subject) because I think this issue is important – and the tone of these letters accurately portrays the surprise and indignation honest, tax paying, law abiding citizens feel when they come to face with the police under these circumstances.

(In view of the fact that important documents have mysteriously disappeared from my possession in the past I should perhaps point out that the original letters I have received are in a secure place and several copies of all the letters have been made and placed in secure places too.)

Time and time again people have written to tell me that the actions of the police have merely made them even more determined to fight on for animals.

Many readers who were caught up in demonstrations by accident (or because they were merely accompanying an enthusiastic pro-animal campaigner) have told me that the actions of the police alerted them to the fact that this is a truly significant issue. The politicians, and the police, will no doubt be disappointed to learn that many of these people – who were not committed pro-animal campaigners when they witnessed police actions – have been converted into pro-animal campaigners by the actions of the police in harassing, assaulting and arresting perfectly innocent protestors.

Cameras Everywhere

Every pro-animal demonstration is filmed by the police (sometimes, I am assured by genuine press photographers, by police photographers in plain clothes who are mixing with press photographers). They use still and video cameras. Helicopters hover overhead and it does not seem unrealistic to assume that they too are equipped with cameras.

From the evidence I have received it seems that the police will sometimes use the information they obtain by photographing (and identifying) individuals and vehicles to harass innocent members of the public who have dared to protest in favour of animal causes.

One woman wrote to me saying: "My son was photographed driving a van near a demonstration. His house has been turned over by seven policemen."

This campaigner, like many others, is banned from going within ten miles of some animal abuse centres – even though he has never been convicted of anything.

Justice?

I sometimes want to weep at the way justice is administered in this country. It seems to me that the word 'justice' doesn't really have anything to do with our legal processes any more. Property is regularly considered far more important than human or animal life.

Recently, for example, a pro-animal campaigner was convicted of setting fire to shops as a protest about the way animals are treated in our society.

The judge told the animal rights activist: "I do accept you did not intend an attack on human life." He then sent the activist to prison for 18 years for presumably assaulting tampons, electric kettles and bottles of aspirin – or whatever else was in the targeted shops.

On the same day a gang of five youths, who called themselves The Young Mafia and who were found guilty of a "long and depraved" gang rape of a 16 year old virgin, were sentenced.

"Some days I feel it would be better if I just went," said the girl, who was previously described as bright and outgoing but was said (not surprisingly) to have become withdrawn and moody. "It would be easier on my family and I would not have to face it any more."

Three of the five gang members received sentences of five years. The other two received 18 month sentences.

Oddly enough, the collected sentences of these five gang members – who wrecked a young girl's life – added up to the same sentence given to the single animal rights supporter who damaged some shops.

A circus worker who was convicted of using an iron bar to give an elephant a vicious and sustained beating was sentenced to four months imprisonment. But a pro-animal campaigner who pleaded guilty to beating a metal fence with a wooden stick, outside a farm where animals were bred for animal experiments, was sent to prison for a year.

What sort of society values a fence more highly than an elephant?

The Truth Is Simple

It seems to me that the truth is simple: pro-animal campaigners are dangerous to the status quo, and to the influential animal abusers who make big profits. I believe the police turn out in huge numbers not because they honestly expect much trouble but simply to try to stop animal rights protests. I suspect the authorities are frightened of long term financial losses rather than short term civil disorder.

The police are mere pawns in the hands of politicians who are themselves controlled by civil servants who are bullied and bribed by industry.

It was, I think, Lenin who wrote that: "to find the culprit see who gains".

In practice I believe that the police in Britain today are being used as though they were the Government's private security force – hired to protect its paymasters.

You and I pay the wages of the police. But the politicians use the police to protect the interests of corporations which have absolutely no interest in our health or welfare. The police in Britain today are protecting evil doers and a corrupt regime just as surely as the police who worked for the white supremacists in South Africa were protecting evil doers and a corrupt regime. Morally, protecting those who abuse animals is little different to protecting those who want to perpetuate apartheid. I believe that the policemen and women who line up to confront pro-animal campaigners are guilty of serious crimes against society, humanity and decency.

Because the average policeman may not be particularly intelligent or well informed and may, indeed, be little more than an authorised thug, there is a tendency for him (or her) to take advantage of the contrived confrontational situation to 'have a bit of fun' and 'break a few heads'. No one seems to make any effort to restrain the police from acting in a wholly insensitive, inappropriate and violent manner. It is my view that far too many policemen and women turn up at pro-animal rallies looking for trouble and action.

Death Threats

As a footnote to all this I think it is worth repeating that I have received many death threats from animal abusers.

In one neatly typed letter the writer (who gave a false name and address) explained in precise and demented detail what would happen to me unless I gave up my campaign to stop scientists performing experiments on animals. The envelope in which the threat arrived also contained a death benefits policy on my life which had been completed with all the appropriate details.

I received a letter from Malta in which the writer told me that he and some fellow hunters were planning to kill me. I sent the letter to the police who asked Interpol to investigate. The police eventually wrote back to tell me that they had not been able to identify the sender of the letter.

At no point was I ever offered police protection. (Nor did I ask for it.) I suspect that if I had been an animal abuser I might have been offered round the clock protection.

The Police As Enemy

The end result of all this is that many people who care about others, who are passionate and kind and sensitive and who want to improve the world in which they live, now regard the police as the enemy. This is sad, dangerous and disturbing. The fact that sane, sensible taxpayers are frightened of the police says more about the police than about the taxpayers.

Meanwhile, the process of marginalisation and misrepresentation continues, with politicians using the police and the media to make the general public believe that those protesting on behalf of animals are dangerous, deluded misfits who love animals more than people.

Controlling The Citizens

Governments have for years now used the drugs war to control their citizens. Fighting drug use has been their constant excuse for spending more money on policing and removing freedom and privacy.

Because they could not use the drugs war excuse to control the internet our politicians devised a new excuse: pornography. And when it became clear that pornography alone was not regarded as a serious enough threat to the survival of the free world the politicians came up with the threat of child pornography. They are now using paedophilia as an excuse for policing computer networks worldwide. (The real irony is that the internet – now regarded by many as a tool for freedom – was originally invented by the US military in case a major nuclear war took out their central military bases.)

Most sensible, Coronation Street viewing, comfortably double glazed citizens used to respond in Pavlovian fashion to talk of government conspiracies and of powerful lobbyists and pressure groups controlling our lives. Conspiracies, they used to think, were part of that world which is populated by people who believe in flying saucers, telepathy, bending spoons and kidnapping by aliens.

But much of that scepticism disappeared when Princess Diana died.

Since then poll after poll has shown that the vast majority of ordinary people believe that Diana was killed. They don't know whether she was killed because she might have been about to marry a Moslem or because of her campaign to ban land mines. But they believe that she was killed and they believe that the British government probably ordered the killing.

Psychiatrists who examined Theodore Kaczynksi (the US Unabomber) said he was convinced: "that every aspect of his existence is controlled by an omnipotent organisation against which he is powerless". The psychiatrists described him as "deeply delusional, paranoid schizophrenic".

But although Kaczynski's response may be described as extreme and anti-social who can argue that his analysis of his condition was not completely accurate?

The Deliberate Marginalisation Of Pro-Animal Campaigners

Politicians in the Soviet Union, the United States of America, Europe and just about everywhere else have for many years dealt with their opponents by 'marginalising' them – or pushing them outside the rest of society by simplifying and falsifying the issues and the facts. Politicians in Britain use this technique in order to control and minimise the effect of those who oppose them, and who might be considered a threat.

The animal abusers (and their supporters) use the media and the police to keep pro-animal campaigners constantly on the defensive, to suppress their views and to push them to the very edges of our society.

Marginalisation is not a new technique. It was used with great effect in the 1930s in the US where steel firm bosses were having a great deal of difficulty with striking steelworkers. Having found that breaking heads and bones tended to antagonise the public, the steel bosses decided to use the media as a subtle alternative. The argument they used was that strikes (and strikers) were hurting everyone. Union activity was equated with communism. Newspapers were used to tell ordinary citizens that the strikers were damaging their future, their children and their country. "Striking is un-American', said the bosses, in what was probably the first sound-bite in history.

The simple but extremely effective technique of marginalisation – which usually relies on triggering an instinctive or emotional response – is used by governments whenever they are at war. Anyone who speaks out against any sort of military conflict will quickly be attacked as being 'against our troops' and 'putting our boys lives in danger'.

During the Gulf War anyone who complained that the war was only being fought to help keep down the price of oil was accused of 'endangering our troops' and of being 'unpatriotic'. Instead of attempting to explain or justify the war the politicians produced and stuck with simple slogans such as 'support our troops'. The electors were not given a chance to discuss the war and anyone who dared to point out that modern wars do seem to break out at convenient times for politicians (when an election is due, when there has been a dip in the polls or when a scandal is breaking) was quickly marginalised as 'unpatriotic'.

The British and the American governments were not the only ones to use marginalisation to good effect during the Gulf War; the Kuwaitis are alleged to have hired public relations experts to spread rumours about the terrible things done by the Iraqis.

Anyone who promotes gay rights will be marginalised as being 'opposed to family values' and 'trying to corrupt the young'. And anyone who speaks out against the war on drugs will be attacked for supporting drug use. A few years ago I wrote a book called *The Drugs Myth* in which I explained in some detail why the drugs war has not worked, does not work and will not work and why the decriminalisation of illegal drugs would result in less drug use and fewer deaths. I was, inevitably, attacked with some venom by many who didn't bother to read the evidence which I had compiled – but merely attacked me for daring to oppose the officially accepted theory that the only way to reduce drug use is to wage war on the streets. I was, said my critics, obviously keen to see more young people taking drugs!

Marginalisation works by turning the rest of the community against the targeted individuals or groups. Protesters and dissidents are made to feel alone; members of a tiny, out of step and insignificant minority. (It is, incidentally, for this reason that politicians and the police – and the controlled areas of the media – usually under-estimate the number of people taking part in a demonstration or public protest.)

'Demonising'

Pro-animal campaigners are marginalised in a number of ways.

The simplest technique used is to 'demonise' pro-animal campaigners by branding all animal lovers and activists as 'violent'. The very word 'activist' is now used in a derogatory way and people have been encouraged to be wary of anyone described as an 'activist'. (I have used the word 'demonise' because it seems appropriate. Journalists who are given the job of trying to make someone seem mad, bad and dangerous – whatever the truth – often describe the technique as 'monstering'.)

Although I have never taken part in or supported any violent activity (and have, indeed, frequently opposed violence and called for animal rights to be won through peaceful means) I have been frequently (and entirely inaccurately and dishonestly) accused of supporting violence. Attempts have, in this (and other ways), been made to marginalise me and reduce the level of any public support I might win through books, articles, broadcasts or speeches.

Marginalising pro-animal campaigners in this way is, of course, rather ironic since most people who care about animals do so because they are peaceful, gentle and sensitive individuals who find it difficult to accept the cruel way in which animals are so often treated. It is, however, for this reason that politicians make sure that pro-animal demonstrations are attended by vast numbers of police officers – often dressed in full riot gear and supported by anti-terrorist style vehicles and helicopters. I do not believe that the police are there because there is any genuine danger of violence. I believe they are there because it serves the politicians' purpose for pro-animal campaigners to be marginalised as violent. The police have been described by one campaigner, as being: "the security guards for institutionalised cruelty". They are more than that; they are an essential part of the marginalisation process.

Total Nonsense

Perhaps the most potent technique used by the opponents of pro-animal campaigners is to claim that anyone who protests on behalf of animals must automatically love animals more than he or she loves people. This is, of course, a total nonsense and anyone who has studied history will know that just about every individual who has campaigned on behalf of animals has also campaigned on behalf of people – and that the vast majority of those who have campaigned on behalf of (and genuinely cared about) people have also campaigned on behalf of animals.

Those who care about animals care because they are sensitive and caring individuals. It is a nonsense to suggest that they might care exclusively about members of another species. But those who use this particular marginalisation technique know that if they say something often enough, and firmly enough, many people will eventually believe them.

The technique is sometimes used with clever (but exceptionally cruel and unjust) refinements. For example, the individual who wishes to marginalise pro-animal campaigners will produce a child, or a photograph of a child, whom they claim has been 'saved' in some way as a result of animal experiments. The implication (which is usually spelt out in precise and heart warming detail) is that the pro-animal campaigner would rather save a rat, a mouse or indeed any animal than save the named child's life. Indeed, it is by no means unknown for the animal abuse supporter to claim that the pro-animal campaigner doesn't care if this (and other) children die. This technique has the added advantage for the animal abuser that while marginalising and brutalising the image of the pro-animal campaigner it also spreads the entirely false and discredited notion that there is a link between animal experiments and saving human lives.

Anyone who dares to oppose animal abuse must expect to be marginalised and demonised (or monstered). I have seen animal abusers claim that individuals who protest on behalf of animals are all dangerous lunatics who are out to overthrow our stable society and will ally themselves with any cause which is a threat to the status quo. I have even seen it said that people who campaign on behalf of animals do not themselves particularly like animals, but have chosen to join the animal rights cause in the absence of any other cause to support. (The argument here is that our society is so perfect that protesting on behalf of animals is the only thing left for those who are irrational and alienated.)

Part Four

"So, What Do We Do Now?"

Chapter One

It Doesn't Have To Be Like This

We can either sit back, watch TV and let the government get on with running (and ruining) the country their way – on behalf of the large corporations which they now represent; or we can protest.

A physical uprising is ruled out because modern governments rule by force and control the media. A modern flag waving, barricade building revolution would last no more than minutes.

But we have to put power back where it truly belongs: in the hearts and minds of people who care.

Outdated Fears And Prejudices

The way that animals are treated, and the ways in which pro-animal campaigners are frequently ignored, constantly marginalised and often victimised are typical examples of much that is wrong with our society.

Our politicians are controlled not by the people who voted them into power (and whose views they were elected to represent) but, to a very large extent, by those with wealth and control of the media. Most important of all, our leaders are now controlled by the social and commercial institutions which we have created.

Most people are too cowed and too easily convinced by outdated prejudices and fears to fight for change.

As J. Howard Moore pointed out back in 1906: "The persistence with which savage ideas and instincts continue to influence men long after those ideas and instincts have really become anachronistic and vestigial is well illustrated by civilised men and women everywhere. The sun continues to 'rise' and 'set' in all civilised lands just as it used to do to the savage, although men have long since learned that it does not do either."

Followers Not Leaders

There once was a time when (at least some) politicians were honest and honourable and led from the front: inspired by personal beliefs and a sense of duty. There was a time when politicians would resign in disgrace and embarrassment if found guilty of wrong-doing or poor judgement. That time has long gone. Today's politicians react rather than act. They believe in expediency rather than integrity. Modern politicians are followers, not leaders, and they adapt their policies (if that is not too grand a word for a disparate set of ever changing prejudices) to fit what they believe will be in the best interests of themselves and their corporate sponsors. These aren't 'real policies' -- they are 'convenience policies'.

Once they have found a 'policy' which their researchers tell them will go down well they sell it like a new brand of soap. Passion and conviction are not words which modern politicians would understand.

Modern politicians may start out with ideals, principles and convictions but they gradually convince themselves that they have to be pragmatic and practical in order to achieve power.

Once they have the power they continue to prevaricate, partly because they are used to it, partly because they have left their principles so far behind that they have forgotten what it means to do something solely because you believe it is the right thing to do, and partly because they have fallen in love with the trappings of power, prestige, fame and success – all of which they are desperate to retain at any cost.

Politicians excuse their failure to act by claiming that if they did act they might prejudice their political careers – neatly and conveniently forgetting the fact that their original reason for acquiring political power was, allegedly at least, to be able to do the very thing they are now saying they cannot do because it might jeopardise their position.

Political parties used to have ideals and principles. Without those essential ingredients all that is left is layer upon layer of half truths and downright lies.

Today's politicians sell the power and responsibility they have been loaned to the corporate sponsors with the deepest pocket.

Next time you are told by an 'official' body that tap water is safe to drink, that all alternative anti-cancer drugs are unsafe and ineffective, that all prescription drugs are thoroughly tested, that a vegetarian diet will lead to nutritional shortages, that heart disease must be treated with drugs or surgery, that chemotherapy, radiotherapy and surgery are the only way to tackle cancer and so on and so on you should remember the track record of official and semi-official organisations.

In the medium and long term we need politicians who will insist that the truth be told.

Our politicians have failed us.

The great political leaders (Lincoln, Churchill and de Gaulle spring to mind as examples) didn't follow polls or focus groups or devote themselves to telling everyone what they believed they wanted to hear. They didn't employ hordes of scriptwriters, advisers, make-up artists and campaign consultants. They didn't have image advisers and they didn't have their teeth capped or their hair dyed. They did have ideas, beliefs and philosophies to offer.

It is hardly surprising that honest, sensitive, thoughtful citizens who do care tend to feel demoralised and despondent and to lose hope in the future.

When footballers behave badly on the field no one is surprised when the fans behave badly on the terraces and in the stands.

When politicians behave dishonestly it is hardly surprising that the nations they lead become devoid of courage and moral fibre.

When politicians do what they think they can get away with, and are driven solely by a need to be re-elected, when they take no notice of what they have promised and are unconcerned with what is right or wrong, it is hardly surprising that there is a general feeling of spiritual malaise.

Political integrity may seem a long way away from endemic social 'depression' but it isn't.

We Need A Battle Plan

Just hoping that things will get better will get us nowhere. The animal abusers (whether they be hunters, vivisectors, butchers or genetic engineers) work well together; drawn together by their evil purposes.

Orthodox political campaigning is utterly pointless. The politicians have shown that they are prepared to make promises which they will break without turning a hair. They do not hesitate to renege on deals they make and have no sense of shame.

Peaceful protest is becoming more and more difficult. Modern politicians do not believe in freedom of speech. Freedom of speech is no longer a right or a reality.

Keeping Your Head Down Isn't An Option

There are, of course, those who would rather be kept in the dark about what is happening in the world. "I feel very depressed about the state of the world," wrote one reader of mine recently. "I agree with you that we can no longer trust politicians, doctors, bureaucrats, food companies, the police, the courts or, indeed, anyone in power. Everywhere I look I see betrayal and deceit. But I don't agree with you when you say that we should all protest. Several of my friends tried protesting – two got arrested, one lost his job and one was thrown out of his rented accommodation because his landlady saw his picture in the local paper and decided that he was a troublemaker. There isn't anything we can do about the way things are. The only answer is to keep your head down, lead a quiet life and hope no one notices you."

I understand that people frequently feel frustrated. Believe me I get angry and frustrated too. I too am sometimes overwhelmed with a sense of despair. I too cry tears of anger, sorrow and frustration.

For over thirty years now I have been harassed, threatened and sued by the people who want to keep on abusing people and animals. My books and advertisements have been banned and I have been fired by newspaper and magazine editors more times than I can remember. (On one occasion an editor fired me with the words: "Your trouble is that you make people think". I liked that. I would be proud to have it as an epitaph.)

The General Medical Council once told me that they got more complaints about me than about any other doctor. None of the complaints came from patients – they all came from drug companies and other individuals and organisations whose nefarious activities I had exposed. In the absence of any other excuse they all wanted me to be struck off for 'advertising'.

I have been endlessly lied about. I have been vilified by government ministers, Department of Health spokesmen, doctors' representatives and numerous other official and quasi official bodies. In every case the complaint has been that I have threatened an industry of some kind. In each case I have, in the long run, been proved right.

It has often been tempting to lock the door, draw the curtains and give up fighting the establishment.

But I can't and I won't.

As long as people who have power cheat and lie, break promises and suppress information that should be available to everyone I will continue to fight to uncover hidden and disguised truths.

It seems to me that it is important that the truth is published and that people can read it. It's important that as many of us as is possible know what is going on and it is also important that the corrupt and the cruel know that we know.

The truth is that we can make a difference. Alone you and I can only make a very small difference. But together we can make a real difference. Together we can change the way things are.

I believe that keeping your head down is selfish and ultimately defeatist. Those who do not protest about the obscenely fascist and grotesquely unfriendly actions of governments and large corporations are just as guilty as the politicians and business executives who are responsible (either consciously or by default) for attempting to turn the entire world into a massive '1984' style Prisoner of War camp.

We have to protest – it is the only worthwhile sign that we are truly free. We have to stand up for what we believe in. We have to make our voices heard. We have to protest about unjust laws. We have to complain about immoral and unethical practices. If we don't stick to our ideals and our values then we lose our pride, our passions and our very reason for living.

Adding Action To Feeling

We really can make a difference.

We must encourage those around us to dust off their principles, drag their dreams back out of the attic and scream and shout and let those in power know that we care.

As William Hazlitt, the great essayist, put it, the purpose of oratory (and politics) is "to build upon the habitual prejudices of mankind (for reason of itself will do nothing) and to add feeling to prejudice and action to feeling."

Today's cheap rate politicians and their advisors believe that complex issues have to be reduced into easily digestible titbits and soundbites. Political parties believe that candidates and policies have to be marketed like commercial products. In our modern, simplistic world journalists look for simple solutions, sound bites rather than philosophies.

A few decades ago Gandhi, when asked what he thought about western civilisation replied that he thought it would be a good idea. Today he would probably add the rider that it also seemed extremely unlikely. We have to change that.

Doing The Right Thing – Whatever The Cost

It is true that an honest man is always in trouble. But what alternative is there if you want to be able to look in the mirror without flinching? Standing up for what you believe isn't an option – it is an integral part of life. If you allow yourself to be cowed into silence by those who do wrong then you too become one of the guilty. Real people are prepared to do the right thing whatever the cost.

How terrible it would be to be old and still wish you were the person you wanted to be. How wonderful to grow into the person you wanted to be – and that others would also like to be.

Sometimes the things you regret the most are the things you don't do.

Many people do not allow the horrors of the world to affect them too deeply. They fear that they would go mad if they did not quickly forget and push aside these terrors.

But the wars, the localised, personalised violence and the sheer cruelty are just a part of it.

It sometimes seems as though the entire insane world has become entirely corrupt. Politicians around the world are found guilty of taking bribes but when found out they steadfastly refuse to apologise. Modern politicians only tell the truth if they have to. The food industry now sells garbage which causes cancer, heart disease and other deadly diseases – and kills more people than Hitler ever did. Why are so many people silent? People who would be deeply ashamed if they had a Mafia hit man in the family will respect a tobacco company employee who, through his work, spends his life trying to kill as many people as possible – and, where death isn't possible, trying to cause as much illness and disability as he can. (The link between tobacco and illness is indisputable, so the more successful the tobacco company is, the more illness and death there will be among those who are targeted as customers.)

Our priorities have become confused. We have lost our way. Children are getting leukaemia and other cancers which could have been prevented. Doctors now do more harm than good.

People hear the messages and read the words but they don't do anything – partly because they can't cope with all the information, partly because the truth is inconvenient (if you believe that cancer is caused by specific foods then you will have to make big changes to your life) and partly because they don't think that what they hear is really going to affect them.

Cigarettes are still sold freely in corner shops, supermarkets and pubs even though they kill millions. Drunk driving continues unabated – despite the slaughter on the roads.

And most people ignore it all.

They blame the politicians. They blame industry. They blame fate.

But too many people never want to take any of the blame themselves. And they don't want to have to do anything themselves either. They have handed over responsibility, washed their hands of the world, and let the politicians take charge. If the politicians don't make the world a better place then it is their fault.

But, of course, nothing does get done because the politicians don't care enough. Modern politicians are, almost by definition, tough, ruthless, dispassionate and uncaring people. The only word they really understand is 'compromise'. Most politicians don't go into politics because they want to make the world a better place (although that, of course, is what they say); they go into politics because it's a good career. Politicians get paid extremely well. And the politicians know that they don't have to deal with the horrors of the world because they know that not enough people care – and have the courage to show that they care. Politicians promise what they think the voters want and deliver what they think they can get away with.

The truth is that it doesn't have to be like this.

It's too easy to say: "You can't change the world". If we don't try we never will. But if we put our hearts into it, and we believe we can win, then we can do anything we want to do. Together we can do it: we can make a difference; we can change the world.

We have to believe that.

If we don't believe then there is no future.

Are you angry? Do you care enough, and are you brave enough, to make your voice heard – and to try and change the world?

Every night – when you go to bed – ask yourself what you've done to fight against injustice, and to help make the world a better place for people and animals.

For a catalogue of Vernon Coleman's books
please write to:

Publishing House
Trinity Place
Barnstaple
Devon EX32 9HJ
England

Telephone	01271 328892
Fax	01271 328768

Outside the UK:

Telephone	+44 1271 328892
Fax	+44 1271 328768

Or visit our websites:

www.vernoncoleman.com
www.lookingforapresent.com
www.makeyourselfbetter.net
www.antivivisection.co.uk
www.vegetariandiet.co.uk